FORTRESS • 81

MAORI FORTIFICATIONS

IAN KNIGHT

ILLUSTRATED BY ADAM HOOK

Series editors Marcus Cowper and Nikolai Bogdanovic

First published in Great Britain in 2009 by Osprey Publishing,
Midland House, West Way, Botley, Oxford OX2 0PH, United Kingdom
443 Park Avenue South, New York, NY 10016, USA
Email: info@ospreypublishing.com

A CIP catalogue record for this book is available from the British Library.

ISBN 978 1 84603 370 4

Editorial by Ilios Publishing, Oxford, UK (www.iliospublishing.com)
Page layout by Ken Vail Graphic Design, Cambridge, UK (kvgd.com)
Typeset in Sabon and Myriad Pro
Index by Michael Parkin
Cartography by The Map Studio, Romsey, UK
Originated by PDQ Media, Bungay, UK
Printed and bound in China through Bookbuilders

09 10 11 12 13   10 9 8 7 6 5 4 3 2 1

FOR A CATALOGUE OF ALL BOOKS PUBLISHED BY OSPREY MILITARY
AND AVIATION PLEASE CONTACT:

NORTH AMERICA
Osprey Direct, c/o Random House Distribution Center, 400 Hahn Road,
Westminster, MD 21157
Email: uscustomerservice@ospreypublishing.com

ALL OTHER REGIONS
Osprey Direct, The Book Service Ltd, Distribution Centre, Colchester Road,
Frating Green, Colchester, Essex, CO7 7DW
E-mail: customerservice@ospreypublishing.com

www.ospreypublishing.com

ACKNOWLEDGEMENTS

Special thanks are due to archaeologist Kevin Jones for use of his excellent
aerial photographs of *pa* sites, to the staff of the National Library of New
Zealand, Te Puna Matauranga O Aotearoa, for their quick and helpful
service, and to Michael Graham-Stewart, not only for the use of the
Ruapekapeka watercolour but for help in liaising with appropriate
individuals and institutions in New Zealand.

ARTIST'S NOTE

Readers may care to note that the original paintings from which the
colour plates in this book were prepared are available for private sale.
All reproduction copyright whatsoever is retained by the Publishers.
All enquiries should be addressed to:

Scorpio Gallery, PO Box 575, Hailsham, E Sussex, UK

The Publishers regret that they can enter into no correspondence upon
this matter.

THE FORTRESS STUDY GROUP (FSG)

The object of the FSG is to advance the education of the public in the study
of all aspects of fortifications and their armaments, especially works
constructed to mount or resist artillery. The FSG holds an annual
conference in September over a long weekend with visits and evening
lectures, an annual tour abroad lasting about eight days, and an annual
Members' Day.

The FSG journal FORT is published annually, and its newsletter Casemate is
published three times a year. Membership is international. For further
details, please contact:

The Secretary, c/o 6 Lanark Place, London W9 1BS, UK

Website: www.fsgfort.com

THE WOODLAND TRUST

Osprey Publishing are supporting the Woodland Trust, the UK's leading
woodland conservation charity, by funding the dedication of trees.

CONTENTS

MAORI FORTIFICATIONS

THE ROLE OF WARFARE IN MAORI SOCIETY

The Maori are a Polynesian people who populated the islands of New Zealand from eastern Polynesia in a series of migrations believed to have taken place at the end of the 13th century. It was popularly held among later Europeans in New Zealand that the Maori had displaced a pre-existing indigenous society but this view has largely been discredited by the lack of archaeological evidence to suggest a previous occupation, and the Maori are now widely regarded as the first human population of the islands. They settled extensively across the most fertile areas of the North Island, and to a lesser extent on the South, subsisting by hunting, fishing and agriculture. Their early impact upon New Zealand's unique species of large flightless birds – notably the Moa –

An early engraving of a pre-colonial fortified village, giving a good impression of the stout palisades and concentric rings of defences. (Author's collection)

was catastrophic, however, and since the islands contained no indigenous animals hunting largely fell away as a viable means of sustenance. Fishing, including the collecting of shellfish, remained an important source of protein, however, together with trapping birds, while the *kumara* or sweet potato assumed the role of a staple cultivated crop. New Zealand flax[1] was used extensively to weave items of clothing, mats and thatching.

Historically, despite a shared sense of common origins traced in Maori mythology to an idealized Polynesian world from which they were descended, the Maori had little sense of a political unity as a people. Instead they defined their identity and allegiance in terms of local 'tribes', *iwi*, or sub-tribes, *hapu*, to which they belonged. Each *iwi* acknowledged a notional descent from common ancestors, identified according to the canoes from which, it was believed, they had arrived in the islands, and was divided into a number of related *hapu*. Each *hapu* was essentially an extended kinship or family group, and it was within the context of the *hapu* that most Maori primarily defined their sense of belonging. Each *hapu* was dominated by a ruling family whose male descendants were recognized as being of a ruling class, *rangatira*. The senior man of this lineage was acknowledged as the *ariki*, a word that roughly corresponds with 'chief' in English usage.

The *hapu* rather than the *iwi* was the dominant political group within pre-colonial Maori society. While each *iwi* identified itself in relationship to a particular territory, each *hapu* within that area settled and administered its own district. Ideally, the territory in which each *hapu* lived gave them access to sufficient natural resources to make them self-sufficient in food production. It was the *hapu* that framed the daily administrative needs of the Maori, and provided a strong infrastructure of mutual support. Although *hapu* within a particular *iwi* often quarrelled and sometimes fought, it was part of their role to set aside differences in the face of a common threat from outside the group.

1 New Zealand flax, *Phormium*, is a distinct species, different from Western Hemisphere flax, *Linum usitatissimum*, but was named 'flax' by early European settlers in New Zealand because of its similar fibrous properties.

The interior of a *pa*; note both the *whares* and raised food stores. Pigs, which feature so prominently in this study of Maori life, were in fact introduced to New Zealand by Europeans. (Author's collection)

The question of land 'ownership' was to be a fraught one throughout Maori history. The Maori had a deep spiritual attachment to their land but little sense of individual ownership. Land was owned collectively by the *hapu*; while it lay within the prerogative of the *rangatira* to apportion the rights to live upon it, it could not be alienated in perpetuity. However, since the boundaries of the territories of individual *iwi*, and even *hapu*, were often ill defined or contested, disputes were commonplace, a situation further exacerbated by the fact that some *hapu* were settled over a wide area, often living among groups associated with different *hapu*. Nor, indeed, were patterns of settlement static, for many Maori groups moved away for months of the year to harvest maturing crops or fish, according to the season.

It was the responsibility of the chiefs to resolve these disputes. Many could be disentangled through patient negotiation but where positions became entrenched armed conflict could ensue. Tensions could further be exacerbated by affronts offered publicly by a chief or his followers to the dignity of another. Important Maori were highly conscious of their personal prestige, expressed in a complex concept known as *mana*. *Mana* was the spiritual manifestation of the importance, authority, power and reputation accrued by individuals through the actions of their daily lives – a reflection of the status they enjoyed within society as a result of their character and deeds, their wisdom, generosity or ferocity as a warrior. *Mana* accrued with age and experience, but any show of disrespect towards individual or tribal *mana* by outsiders was considered a heinous offence. Infringements of *mana* were the major justification of *utu* – the pursuit of a repayment, revenge – which might wipe out the slur. *Utu* might be claimed not only from the original transgressor but from a member of his family or even *hapu*, and neither did it need to be exacted immediately; it was perfectly acceptable to claim *utu* ten or 20 years later, should the opportunity present itself, from a descendant who had not been alive at the time of the original slight. Often the invocation of the right of *utu* provoked a reprisal in return from those on the receiving end locking groups in a cycle of revenge and retribution that endured for decades. This exacerbated existing political divisions and left Maori society dangerously divided against itself in the face of a concerted threat from outside the islands. During their conquest of New Zealand in the 19th century, Europeans often astutely exploited rivalries among different Maori groups, persuading Maori to fight with them against other Maori. At the time of its greatest test, Maori society would prove unable to offer a united military front in its own defence.

Although the Maori had no concept of a professional army, the need to defend territory, to pursue feuds and to accrue *mana* meant that Maori men grew up in a society influenced by a strong warrior ethic. Nor, indeed, was warfare an exclusively masculine preserve – Maori history is full of examples of resolute women who joined their men in battle in defence of their *hapu*. Fighting men were known as *toa*, and had learned their skills in an active outdoor environment since

A sketch, by George French Angus, of Maori performing a dance outside a *pa* in the 1840s. Note the high palisade supports and the ornate carving above the gateway (right). Many pre-European *pa* were constructed to take advantage of natural defensive features, including rivers and lakes. (Author's collection)

childhood. Since *toa* accrued *mana* in deeds of personal daring, courage and ferocity, Maori warfare was largely individualistic and conducted at close quarters. Indeed, lacking a metal technology, the pre-colonial Maori possessed few long-range weapons apart from the wooden spear and a whip-propelled dart, neither of which was considered particularly worthy of a true warrior. Most *toa* much preferred a variety of two-handed wooden striking weapons – chiefly the *taiha* and *tewhatewha* – and sharp hand-clubs known as *patu* made of wood, bone or green-stone.

In traditional Maori society, the summer months – November, December and January – were the time best suited for campaigning, after crops were planted and before they were harvested. This season was dedicated to Tu, the god of war. Men mustered for war in defence of threats to the territory of their *hapu* or in response to insults to their *mana*. Although the assembled *toa* of a *hapu* served as a battlefield unit, there was no formal organization and battles in the open consisted of an exchange of ritual challenges followed by a mêlée of individual combats. Although the *rangatira* were expected to demonstrate leadership in warfare, they had no authority to compel *hapu* members to fight, and their ability to command depended largely upon their personal *mana* and charisma. Chiefs who displayed courage, skill and determination enjoyed a high level of support among their followers; those who were hesitant or inept found that their support ebbed away. Nevertheless, the Maori generally remained loyal to the idea that the *rangatira* were their natural commanders until, near the very end of the long cycle of wars against Europeans, when the structures of Maori society themselves were under threat of collapse, commoners began to emerge as leaders on the strength of their abilities alone.

CHRONOLOGY

6 February 1840	Treaty of Waitangi signed between British Governor William Hobson and a number of important Maori chiefs. European settlement prior to this date had occurred largely without regulation, and the Treaty marks Britain's first serious attempt to extend its authority into New Zealand. It also marked the start of sponsored British immigration to the islands.
17 June 1843	The Wairau Incident. Settlers from Nelson in the north of the South Island clashed with Ngati Toa Maori under Te Ruaparaha and Te Rangihaeata – the first serious blood shed in the war over land ownership in New Zealand.
8 July 1844	Northern chief Hone Heke cuts down the British flagpole outside the village of Kororareka, Bay of Islands; it is put back up and cut down several times.
11 March 1845	Hone Heke sacks Kororareka.
8 May 1845	British troops respond by attacking Heke's *pa* at Puketutu.
12 June 1845	Pro-British chief Tamati Waka Nene defeats Heke at Te Ahuahu.
1 July 1845	British troops attack Ohaeawai *pa* but are repulsed.
31 December 1845	British troops invest the *pa* built by Heke's ally Kawiti at Ruapekapeka; after days of bombardment it was abandoned by the defenders and occupied by the British on 11 January 1846

2 April 1846	Two settlers killed by Maori in the Hutt Valley near Wellington.
16 May 1846	British outpost attacked at Boulcott's Farm.
6–10 August 1846	British troops attack Te Rangihaeata's *pa* at Horokiri. The defenders abandoned it without being captured.
18 April 1847	Settlers killed near Wanganui. Sporadic fighting continues in the area until July.
March 1859	The disputed 'Waitara Purchase' leads to British troops being deployed in Taranaki to protect surveyors and settlers. Fighting breaks out in March 1860.
27 June 1860	Failed British attack on the Puketakauere *pa*.
6 November 1860	Attack on Maori positions at Mahoetahi.
29 December 1860	Troops under General Pratt build the first of a series of redoubts on the way to the *pa* at Te Arei; the British advance over the following four weeks was accomplished by way of a large sap protected by several redoubts. Once it drew close to Te Arei the Maori negotiated a ceasefire.
12 July 1863	British troops enter the Waikato district on the pretence that Waikato chiefs had supported Maori resistance in Taranaki.
17 July 1863	First action of the Waikato campaign at Koheroa.
14 September 1863	A British outpost at Pukekohe East Church withstands a determined Maori attack.
3 October 1863	Renewed fighting in Taranaki; attack on British position at Allen's Hill.
October 1863	British troops bypass Maori positions at Mere Mere on the Waikato River.
20 November 1863	British attack the position at Rangiriri; the *pa* surrenders in confused circumstances the following morning.
November 1863– February 1864	Fighting in the Waikato Valley.
January 1864	Unrest in Tauranga district.
31 March 1864	First attack on Rewi's *pa* at Orakau. On 2 April the Maori abandoned their position and were harried by British troops in their retreat.
6 April 1864	Captain Thomas Lloyd killed at Kaitake in the Taranaki, and his head used to encourage resistance; start of fighting involving the 'Hau Hau' movement.
29 April 1864	Costly British attack on Pukehinahina in Tauranga – the Gate *pa*.
30 April 1864	Hau Hau attack on Sentry Hill, Taranaki. Beginning of guerilla warfare in south Taranaki and Wanganui.
14 May 1864	Fight between pro- and anti-Hau Hau Maori at Moutoa Island.
21 June 1864	British surprise Maori building a *pa* at Te Ranga in the Tauranga district and inflict heavy casualties on them.
24 January 1865	British attack Nukumaru.

14 January 1866	British troops attack Otapawa *pa*, Wanganui district.
2 March 1865	Rev. Carl Volkner murdered by Chief Kereopa at Opotiki.
November 1865	Hau Hau *pa* at Waeranga-a-Hika invested and captured on 22 November.
9 June 1868	Settlers killed in south Taranaki; start of resistance by Nga Ruahinerangi chief Titokawaru.
4 July 1868	Te Kooti Arikirangi – taken prisoner in earlier fighting – escapes with 300 prisoners from exile in the Chatham Islands. He lands near Poverty Bay; start of Te Kooti campaign.
12 July 1868	Titokawaru's followers attack Turuturumokai Redoubt.
10 August 1868	First British assault against Titokawaru's *pa* at Te Ngutu o te Manu; Further assaults take place on 21 August and 7 September.
7 November 1868	Attack on Titokawaru's position at Moturoa.
10 November 1868	Te Kooti attacks settlements near Poverty Bay.
5 January 1869	Attack on Te Kooti's *pa* at Ngatapa.
1 February 1869	Attack on Tauranga-Ika; the *pa* was abandoned shortly afterwards by the defenders, apparently because of a loss of Titokawaru's *mana*.
March–April 1869	Raids by Te Kooti in the Hawke's Bay district.
4 October 1869	Colonial troops capture Te Kooti's Te Porere *pa* – the last engagement involving Maori fortifications during the New Zealand Wars. Te Kooti continued to resist until 1872 when he took refuge with supporters in the 'King Country'. The New Zealand Government pardoned him in 1883.

THE PRE-COLONIAL *PA*; THE FORTIFIED VILLAGE

Because of the potential for endemic conflict, the need for defence was fundamental to Maori settlement patterns. Although villages were sited close to natural resources – rivers or lakes for water and fish, fertile ground to grow crops, woodland for timber and as a habitat for birds to hunt – the exact choice of location was often dictated by tactical concerns. At the heart of most settlements was a fortified enclosure known as a *pa*. In areas troubled by on-going disputes, the villages themselves were fortified and the defensive works encompassed the homes of the occupants; in more settled areas, the *pa* was a separate enclosure built close to the people's homes but to which they could retire quickly in times of trouble. The *pa*, moreover, formed the psychological cornerstone of community security, embodying the willingness of a *hapu* to defend both its members and its land. While some smaller *hapu*, numbering perhaps a few dozen members, might combine with other *hapu* of their *iwi* to build and occupy a single *pa*, larger *hapu* might build a *pa* to themselves or, if the population required it, several *pa* at key points about their territory. The remaining earthworks of thousands of pre-European *pa* were still to be seen across New Zealand's North Island in the early 20th century – although many have since succumbed to intensive farming methods – testifying to the Maori's long association with the land. In some areas, where a combination of security

A sketch by Angus of the *whare* of the Ngati Toa chief Te Rangihaeata, who played a prominent part in the fighting of the 1840s. His rank is suggested by the degree of ornate carved decoration – a reflection of the greater access many Maori enjoyed by that time to European metal tools. (Author's collection)

and natural resources made for comfortable living, hundreds of *pa* were built, each to be occupied at different times, abandoned and replaced; in other, less hospitable areas, there are very few remains.

The extent and characteristics of Maori settlements made a deep impression upon some of the first European visitors to the islands. Captain James Cook, who visited New Zealand three times between 1769 and 1777, left the first detailed written descriptions of the Maori *pa* he encountered, as did his officers, all of whom were struck by the skill and robustness with which such fortified villages had been built. Of one abandoned *pa* Cook visited near Mercury Bay in November 1769 he wrote,

> A little within the entrance of the river, on the east side, is a high point or peninsular jutting out into the river, on which are the remains of one of their fortified towns. The situation is such that the best engineer in Europe could not have chose a better for a small number of men to defend themselves against a greater; it is strong by nature, and made more so by art. It is only accessible on the land side and there have been cut a ditch, and a bank raised on the inside. From the top of the bank to the bottom of the ditch was about twenty-two feet, and the depth of the ditch on the land-side fourteen feet; its breadth was in proportion to its depth, and the whole seems to have been done with great judgement. There had been a row of pickets on top of the bank, and another on the outside of the ditch; these last had been set deep in the ground and sloping with their upper ends hanging over the ditch.[2]

Of an occupied *pa* known as Wharekaro in the same district – a settlement clearly living in a state of some tension – Cook's botanist, Joseph Banks, noted,

> The whole hill was enclosed by a palisade about ten feet high, made of strong poles bound together with withies: the weak side next to the hill had also a ditch, twenty feet in depth, nearest the palisade. Besides this, beyond the palisade, was built a fighting stage. … It is a flat stage covered with branches

2 Captain Cook, quoted in Elsdon Best, *The Pa Maori*, Wellington, 1927.

10

of trees upon which they stand to throw darts or stones at their assailants, they themselves being out of danger. Its dimensions were as follows: Its height above the ground 20½ ft., breath six feet six inches, length 43 ft.; upon it were laid bundles of darts, and heaps of stones: ready in case of an attack. … The side next to the road was also defended by a similar stage, but much longer; the other two by the steepness thought to be sufficiently secure with the palisade. The inside was divided into, I believe, twenty larger and smaller divisions, some of which contained not more than one or two houses, others twelve or fourteen. Every one of these was enclosed by its own palisade, though not so high and strong as the general one; in these were vast heaps of dried fish and fern roots piled up, so much that if they had water, I should have thought them well prepared for a siege, but that had to be brought from a brook below …[3]

Maori girls preparing flax mats; a typical scene of domestic life within an early *pa*.

These settlements visited by early European travellers varied considerably in size. The Maori population of New Zealand had perhaps already peaked by the 1770s, and was certainly in decline throughout the 19th century. Yet, while many *pa* probably housed no more than a few hundred warriors – and of course their families – others could comfortably contain as many as 2,000 warriors, together with a non-combatant population many times that. Stockades as much as two kilometres in circumference were not exceptional.

Yet Banks' account astutely identifies both the strengths of the key elements of Maori fortifications – the careful use of land, the impressive ditches, robust palisades and defensive towers – but also its more subtle and significant limitations. The almost total lack of long-range weapons worked greatly in favour of the style of defences favoured by the Maoris since it curtailed the options of the attackers and dictated the requirements of the defenders. While an attacker standing even 100m from a *pa* could do so in almost complete impunity, there was almost nothing he could do in return to injure a defender behind a palisade, much less damage or destroy the palisade itself.

Moreover, the nature of Maori society itself meant that protracted sieges, on the European model, were extremely difficult to sustain. The Maori were only part-time warriors, released temporarily from their primary social roles, the need to protect and feed their families. It was seldom that a *hapu* or even an *iwi* was able to raise sufficient men to completely invest a rival *pa* for any length of time; men could not themselves be provisioned indefinitely, and any tactical stalemate worked to the advantage of the defenders. Only if the inhabitants of a *pa* were caught by surprise was there a realistic chance of starving them into submission, and the occasions on which this occurred were sufficiently rare for them to pass into Maori folklore.

3 Banks, Sir Joseph, *Journal During Captain Cook's First Voyage*, London, 1897.

It was perhaps for this reason, and perhaps for the difficulties in incorporating a free-flowing source of water securely within a *pa*, that few of them were equipped with a reliable water supply. Instead, when an attack was expected, water was collected from a nearby source and carried into the *pa* to be stored in gourds or in waterproof pits dug within the defences. This weakness, not altogether apparent in pre-colonial times, would nonetheless make the *pa* acutely vulnerable to the more rigorous tactics employed by Europeans.

The construction of a pre-colonial *pa*

Although all Maori *pa* in pre-European times were guided by the same principles of construction, no two examples were ever alike. The design of each one was dictated by the lie of the land, while the particular combination of trenches, ramparts and palisades was conditioned by the need of its individual designers. As Eldon Best put it, in his classic study *The Pa Maori*:

In studying the fortified positions constructed by the old time Maori, regularity of design must not be expected. The Maori engineer was no disciple of Vauban, he followed no hard and fast system of fortification, he did not mark out his lines of defence from prepared plans. He knew nothing of bastion and gorge, of casemate and embrasure, these things lay in the womb of time, his descendants were to know them in the days that lay before. Nor did he ponder as to where to lay off his curtains and demilune, or how to work in an orthodox terreplein and barbette. He simply selected a suitable site, then studied its contour lines and surroundings, until, with no help of pen or paper, he had grasped the solution to the problem, and worked out his plan. He then proceeded to mark the lines of scarp and fosse, of rampart and stockade, after which he set his men to work and superintended their labours. At certain weak places he threw in an extra stockade or fosse, or erected an elevated platform to command it. The entrance passage he laid off by narrow and tortuous ways flanked by strong defences. According to the contour of the ground, and relative levels, he devised a defence of scarp and stockade, or of fosse and parapet. He cunningly carved a hill into terraces of unequal sizes and levels, each of which became a defensive area in itself. The easiest approach to the fort possessed the strongest defences, and for an enemy to reach the summit area

BOTTOM LEFT
Aerial view of Maungakiekie, One Tree Hill, Auckland. A pre-colonial *pa* built on the lip of an extinct volcano; the terracing and extensive defensive ditches can clearly be seen. (Kevin L Jones/New Zealand Department of Conservation)

BOTTOM RIGHT
Aerial view of Karangaumu, a pre-European *pa* near Papamoa, Bay of Plenty. A number of separate platforms encircled by ditches are clearly visible; the site commands a view of more than 20km of the surrounding coastal plain. (Kevin L Jones/New Zealand Department of Conservation)

meant most strenuous fighting to reduce the various fortified sub-divisions.[4]

The first element in the process was the selection of the ground itself. Although *pa* were sometimes built on level ground, it was far more common, as the above suggests, for them to be built on hilltops. It did not matter if the chosen spot was overlooked by a nearby feature; in the days before gunpowder there was no means of reaching the defences from a distance. An ideal hill was one with naturally guarded approaches, with steep sides or broken cliffs on one or more sides which would shape the approach of an enemy within predictable routes. The proximity of a water source was important for both everyday life and defence, and *pa* were sometimes built on headlands folded round by rivers, or jutting out into lakes. Indeed, among groups living on a lakeside a natural island was an obvious choice on which to site a *pa* since it could be easily fortified, and the defenders could withdraw to it by canoe. Any attack on such a position could be rendered almost impossible by careful defence of the landing areas.

An early 20th-century reconstruction of a traditional 'fighting stage' of a pre-musket period *pa*. (Author's collection)

The presence of wood near a settlement had more ambiguous connotations; often *pa* built in forest areas were not so well constructed as those in open country, for the simple reason that the forest itself offered a place of refuge. Some *hapu* living in densely forested areas preferred to rely on the thickness of the bush for protection, rather than upon fortification. On the other hand, timber was essential for the building of palisades, and to construct a *pa* too far from a forest entailed tremendous physical labour in dragging in the necessary quantity of felled trees.

Hard manual work was, indeed, the main characteristic of the process of constructing a *pa*. The Maori possessed no wheeled transport and no metal tools. Broadly, the design of *pa* fell into two categories – the *pa tuwatawata*, in which the defences were largely limited to wooden palisades, and the more impressive *pa whakairo*, which consisted of deep trenches, ramparts and palisades in various combinations. In either case, the task of moving huge quantities of soil and cutting, transporting and erecting hundreds of heavy wooden posts had to be carried out by hand. It was achieved by the men of the *hapu*, working together in labour gangs, directed by their chief and his advisers.

Often, the work involved a major re-shaping of the contours of a hill itself. Once the lines of defences had been marked out, the summit was usually levelled to provide a flat living area, and terraces cut into the sides, between the defensive lines. These defences – either palisades or trenches alone, or, more usually, both in combination – were built around the perimeter in several rows. In an example employing trenches, these were usually deep, a minimum of two metres, but sometimes three or four metres. The displaced earth was piled up inside to provide a rampart immediately above the trench. Often this was shaped so as to add to the natural scarp of the hill, so that the hill itself took the form of a series of steep slopes and ditches.

4 Best, *The Pa Maori.*

A A pre-colonial *pa*

Before the widespread use of firearms, the Maori had developed a complex system of engineering that made their settlements almost invulnerable to attack by fellow Maori. This *pa* has been built on a knoll surrounded by a natural defensive feature, a stream. The knoll itself has been terraced to provide living areas and encircled by ramparts and ditches. The outer stockade is particularly strong, and is screened by an extra row of inward leaning palisades. The main gateway is screened by an outer palisade and guarded by a tall fighting tower; other fighting towers protect vulnerable parts of the defences. As the insets show, fighting towers allowed the defenders to reach down with long spears and strike at defenders exposed in the open near the palisades. Paths through the settlement passed through the inner stockades at irregular intervals to prevent attackers exploiting a single entry point. The construction of such a *pa* required a huge physical effort; earth was moved with a variety of wooden spades and shovels, and the great timber supports of the palisades had to be dragged manually into place and sunk into holes by means of a scaffold. Note the stylized human figures carved at irregular intervals into the larger stockade supports. Although attempts were sometimes made by attackers to tear down the stockades by tossing a log tied to a rope among them and hauling on the rope, this was seldom successful; on the rare occasions when *pa* were carried it was usually by stealth or by fire.

All of this soil was broken up and moved by means of a number of simple wooden implements. These included the *wauwau*, a pointed stick used to break up the soil, the *ko*, a stout stick about two metres in length and pointed at one end with a foot-rest inserted near the point, and used like a spade, and the *koko*, a hand shovel made out of a section of tree-bark. To accomplish these impressive tasks men often worked in unison, chanting work-songs. The removed earth was piled up on the inside by hand until the rampart grew too high; then it was passed up to men working above by means of baskets of woven flax.

As a result, the ramparts often rose to a height of three metres above the bottom of the trench, and sometimes, in major works, as much as four or five. To prevent the earth from collapsing from its own weight, it might be bound together with vegetation such as flax, bracken or *manuka* brush. There were no *banquettes* or firing steps in pre-colonial Maori *pa* because the Maori had no long-range weapons suited for use from behind a rampart; instead, the ramparts were upwards of two metres thick at the top, and flattened to allow the defenders to move along or stand on them to fight. From the top of a high rampart, jabbing down with long wooden spears up to six metres long, the defenders enjoyed an almost unchallenged advantage over attackers struggling through the ditch and up the steep scarp below.

There was no preferred number of trenches and ramparts around the perimeter of a *pa*. It was unusual to have less than two – an outer screen and a main line of defence – while some major works had as many as four. In some cases two or three lines of ramparts and trenches were constructed in quick succession up a slope, with just a few metres between them to allow for the movements of the defenders; in others, there might be two lines quite close together, with further lines built within areas of terracing and nearer to the summit. Generally, however, one line had deeper and wider trenches and higher ramparts than the others and was considered the main line, with the others serving as supports. Although it was common for the lines to completely surround the settlement, this was dependant upon the lie of the land, and in cases where the *pa* was built on a prominence that fell away on some side into steep cliffs, the ramparts were sometimes built up to the edge of the cliff, so that the face itself formed the main defensible feature on that side.

It was on the terraces inside the defences that ordinary dwellings were built. These were generally grouped according to family or kinship needs, but beyond that early white visitors saw nothing comparable to the streets that divided houses in European towns. The homes themselves were known as *whares*, and consisted of single-storey dwellings of flax thatching erected over a wooden frame. The *whares* themselves were primarily sleeping areas, while food was prepared in communal cooking huts. The area occupied by each family group was often surrounded by a light palisade, so that although there were recognizable paths leading from the main entrance to all areas of the settlement, these were seldom direct in order to prevent an enemy striking easily into the heart of a settlement. On the terraced summit of the hill was an area usually reserved for the occupation of the leaders of the *hapu* and somewhere nearby was a communal hall and an open meeting space. There are references, too, to communal food-stores being placed near the centre of the *pa*. When the work was a fortified village, permanently occupied due to the unsettled nature of the country, crops were either grown close outside the perimeter, or, if space allowed, within the settlement itself. Underground storage pits were dug to stockpile *kumara* sweet potatoes, and waterproof pits were also dug to store water, which were filled from rivers or streams nearby if an attack was threatened. As Joseph Banks noted, dried fish might also be stockpiled in anticipation of an attack.

Perhaps the most distinctive aspect of the pre-colonial *pa*, however, was its impressive rows of wooden palisades. Four types of palisade were widely recognized, the *pekerangi* or outer screen, the *wita* or second line, the *katua* or *tuwatawata*, the third or main line of defence, and the *parakiri* or innermost line of defence. Only the most thoroughly built *pa* was likely to include all four stockades, although very few did not include both the *pekerangi* and *katua*. These palisades were usually constructed in conjunction with the trenches and ramparts, although it was not unknown for *pa* to be built with palisades only. Often the stockades were built on the top of the trenches, crowning them with a further extremely difficult obstacle, and indeed it was unusual for the *pekerangi* not to be placed on the outer ramparts, above the perimeter trench; sometimes, however, ramparts were left without palisades, or palisades built between the lines of ramparts.

Stockades were made by setting large supporting posts in a line at intervals of roughly two metres. These posts were usually made of a hardwood such as *puriri* (*Vitex lucens*), which, while extremely difficult to work with stone tools, was durable and famously resistant to weathering. These main posts varied considerably in size, averaging between three and four metres, and had a diameter of perhaps 20 or 30cm. The posts had to be felled in the nearest forest, trimmed and then dragged to the *pa* site by hand. This in itself required considerable communal effort on the part of the *hapu*'s men folk, as the raw logs were lashed at the top and bottom with ropes made of creeper then dragged across country. Since the Maori had no means of hammering them in place, holes were dug in the selected spots and a wooden buttress erected; they were then hauled into place by ropes thrown over a scaffold built for the purpose, and the hole filled around them and the earth compacted.

A beautifully crisp aerial photo of Mokai a Tonga, a pre-European *pa* near Wanganui. Note the combination of double ditches and ramparts. (Kevin L Jones/New Zealand Department of Conservation)

In the main line of the stockade, the *katua*, the tops of these posts were roughly shaped into blocks. This symbolized the ancient practise of mounting the severed heads of enemy dead upon the palisades as a gesture of defiance. Often, within a particularly significant *pa*, every fifth or sixth post was particularly large. It would commonly be two or three metres higher than the average post, and in some cases these taller posts were as much as ten metres high. They were also thicker than average, for the top portion – perhaps two metres high – was ornately carved into a stylized representation of a human form in typically Maori style. These figures were said to represent significant personalities or ancestors among the *hapu* and their faces, heavily etched with *moko*, the spiralling facial tattooing characteristic of the Maori fighting man in life, usually bore expressions of foreboding or anger. The eyes were sometimes set with shells, and the figures often painted a deep, dark red. They were set looking outwards, over the top of the outer palisades and towards the enemy.

Lashed horizontally to these supporting posts were long rails, usually lengths of the stem of selected climbing plants. These stems were split and cut into appropriate lengths. They were lashed to the support poles with a type of tough creeper. In the outer palisade, and in the principal one, there were usually three such rails parallel to one another, while in the secondary palisades just two. These rails formed the supports for the rows of upright palings that fenced the stockade between the larger support posts. These palings were made from roughly split wood and were perhaps ten or 12cm wide. No attempt was made to ensure any regularity in the length, and they were usually at about three metres high – tall enough to comfortably shelter a man standing – and individual pieces might be considerably longer. They were tied to the rails by lengths of creeper lashed diagonally around them or crossed at the back. A gap of ten centimetres or so was left between each paling, so that in battle men standing behind them could thrust their spears comfortably through at an attacker.

Some particularly well-constructed *pa* included refinements on these basic principles. Sometimes, when the defences included a steeply sloping piece of ground, the outer palisade was built at an angle, leaning outwards at the top, so that an attacker would not only have to struggle up the scarp itself but then be faced with a line of defenders secure behind a palisade hanging out above their heads. Many *pa* also included a *wita*, a light outer barrier in which the pales were bound as usual to cross-rails but did not extend all the way to the ground. This form of defence, known as *aparua*, was constructed just a metre or so in front of the outer defended stockade, and served to delay the enemy within range of long thrusting weapons held by the defenders. The gaps between and below the posts were a deliberate feature to deprive the attacker of any potential shelter. In some cases the *wita* inclined inwards at the top, where the points of the posts were bound to the main palisade. This made it almost impossible for an attacker to tear down the *wita*, and any attempt to scale it would leave their bodies hopelessly exposed to the defenders behind the main barrier.

The French traveller, Crozet, described another very significant feature of the pre-European *pa* in 1772:

> Inside the village, at the side of the gate, there is a sort of timber platform about 25ft. high, the posts being about 18 in. to 20 in. in diameter and sunk solidly in the ground. The people climb onto this sort of advance post by means of a post with foot-steps cut into it. A considerable collection of stones

and short javelins is always kept up there, and when they fear an attack they picket the sentinels there. The platforms are roomy enough to hold fifteen or twenty fighting-men.[5]

It was common for a *pa* to include one or more of these platforms, known variously as *puhara*, *puwhara* or *pourewa*. Some might be of considerable length, and Joseph Banks measured one with a frontage of 13m. One was usually built near the gateway, to provide an extra level of defence against that obvious point of attack. Others might be built to command a piece of particularly dead ground on the approaches to the outer palisade. The usual method of construction was to set four large posts upright in the ground. A frame was made by lashing horizontal cross-pieces as supports, and these were 'floored' with pales laid in the opposite direction. Although sometimes the defenders merely stood upon these floors, exposed to such enemy missiles as there were, it was more common to erect a light screen on each side to provide a protective wall. Access to the platform was by means of a single log, carved with steps, at the rear. As Crozet's account suggests, piles of stones were usually kept on the platforms to hurl down at attackers, and they were also defended by men armed with long spears who could jab downwards at attackers struggling over the various obstacles below and in front of them.

As with all things connected with the Maori art of fortification, there were a number of variations on the concept of the elevated platform, too. The *kotaretare* was a smaller stage in which the palisade itself provided the front supports, and the floor projected forward above it. Defenders on this stage were therefore standing directly over the heads of any attackers approaching the palisade itself. Platforms were occasionally built using an appropriate single tree, with the branches cut into a shape and the floor built between them. Other accounts mention small platforms made from a single pole, with the floor lashed on either side and the usual stepped log serving as a ladder; such platforms might only support one or two men, but their presence at a crucial angle in the defences could be decisive.

Another function of these platforms was to serve as a lookout tower, and at times when an attack was expected sentries would be placed upon them at night, beating regularly on a hollow log to sound the 'all's well', to reassure the inhabitants and warn any approaching enemy.

One aspect of the *pa* that not unnaturally received considerable attention was the *kuwaha*, or main entrance. The entrance was usually through various rows of palisades and entrenchments, and was generally made as difficult as possible for a potential attacker to break through. The various gateways between these rows were not generally aligned with each other, and the paths between them wound through houses and screened gardens, and below and alongside inner ramparts, enabling the

A young Maori man with a long wooden spear. Such weapons were the mainstay of the defence of *pa* in the pre-colonial period. (Author's collection)

5 *Crozet's Voyage to Tasmania, New Zealand etc*, London 1891.

defenders to make a stand at any point. The first entrance, through the outer defences, was usually screened to provide a narrow passage, known as an *ngutu*. This was made by placing a screen – either palisades or ramparts – directly in front of the entrance or inside it, within the defences. In either case any attackers would be funnelled around this screen, approaching the gateway through narrow points, and all the while exposed to the attentions of the defenders. Sometimes the screen was attached at one end to the palisade, so that the *ngutu* was in effect a long alleyway stretching from outside the *pa* along the length of part of the stockade to the gate within, defended each step of the way. It was not unknown for this alleyway to pass directly under a raised fighting platform before finally emerging into the interior.

Usually, there was no gap in any outer trenches to allow the occupants to pass over them – instead they provided themselves with two or three sturdy logs to serve as a bridge. These of course could easily be pulled up at night or during an attack, and hurdles of interwoven saplings blocked the gateways themselves. The principle gateway to the *pa* was considered to be the entrance through the main stockade (usually the second rather than front row). This was often framed with two large long poles bearing particularly impressive carved figures. Sometimes the gap between these figures was blocked by fencing, apart from a low hole, big enough for a man to crawl through; sometimes this hole was simply cut through the base of a single large tree-trunk which was itself decorated with intricate carvings of human figures. Occasionally the entrance to the inner compartments was by means of a tunnel, dug through the ramparts. Tunnels, indeed, were a common feature of the pre-European *pa*, and in extreme examples they were constructed as an escape feature, providing a secret means of passing through one or more lines of defence and leading out to a patch of forest or a riverbank beyond.

For the most part, as already noted, the typical Maori *pa* usually had no access to free-running water within the defences. *Pa* were usually built a few hundred metres from streams, rivers or lake shores, however, because water was obviously essential to the daily peacetime life of the inhabitants. When an attack threatened, the inhabitants would simply collect water in gourds and carry it up the hillside into the defences for storage. Sometimes pits were dug between the ramparts to serve as reservoirs; these were lined with wood, filled by hand and replenished by rainwater running down the trenches. More often troughs were cut from large logs and used to store water.

Sanitation was also a concern, especially if a *pa* could expect to be the subject of a prolonged attack. During peacetime people used as latrines specific spots away from the defences of the *pa* itself, but when under attack areas within the defences were set aside for the purpose. Sometimes they would be built on the edge of a natural feature incorporated into the defences, such as above a cliff-face or ravine; sometimes a tunnel was cut through the defences leading to the outside. The latrines themselves consisted of a log suspended over the pit or edge, screened with light palisades for privacy.

Ceremonial aspects of the *pa*

The success of a *pa* in achieving the security and safety of its occupying *hapu* was considered to be due as much to the adherence to religious ritual as to the skill of its engineers. A *pa* itself had *mana*, which reflected not only the reputation of its occupants but the respect with which it had been built. The erection of the first post was a significant moment enshrined in ceremony; the post had to be hauled upright during the morning while a leading member of the *hapu* stood on the scaffold erected for the purpose and chanted a religious *tau* or song. People hearing the song were required to remain quiet and refrain from chores while the post was hauled into place. A similar ceremony accompanied the erection of all the corner posts of the main stockade. Very occasionally, the construction of a new *pa* was blessed by the capture and execution of an individual from a rival group – although this practise was probably always rare, and does not seem to have survived into European times. It was, however, an almost universal practise, even in the wars of the 19th century, to bury in the heart of the *pa* a stone, known as a *mauri* or *whatu*, which served to focus the protection of the various deities or ancestors whose blessing was sought for the work.

The work of constructing a *pa* fell to the men of a *hapu*, and during the time that they were employed upon it they were the subject of a *tapu*, a religious proscription. Women could not enter the fortifications until they were completed and the *tapu* lifted, for fear of irrevocably tainting its *mana*. Once the defences were built and the first house within the *pa* constructed a ceremony was held to lift the *tapu* in which a young woman from one of the *hapu*'s leading families passed through the main gateway to the accompaniment of religious chants from an officiating priest.

Attacking and defending the pre-colonial *pa*

In pre-colonial times, so generally understood were the basic tenets of fortification that an attacker, even if they knew nothing of the particular defences of an individual *pa*, nevertheless recognized the difficulties with which they were likely to be faced. If possible, therefore, they attempted to carry an enemy fortification by some means other than direct assault, as this was always likely to be the most costly and least successful option.

The first option was to take the objective by surprise. Generally an attacking force tried to infiltrate enemy territory by stealth, unnoticed, and it sent scouts ahead to test out the defences. Very occasionally their arrival was entirely unexpected, and the enemy were attacked as a result before they could take refuge in their *pa*. This was unusual, however, if only because once conflict seemed likely the defenders were on the look out for signs of attack. When an enemy force was reported in the vicinity, the defenders immediately abandoned any outlying settlements and retired to their *pa*, taking with them whatever foodstuffs – including crops hurriedly harvested in the fields, whether ripe or not – and water they could gather. The men put the defences in good order, clearing any ditches that had filled with rubbish and repairing weathered stockades, the roofs of the *whares* within were piled over with soil to reduce their vulnerability to fire, and the gateways blocked. If no attack was forthcoming straight away, watchmen were posted on the raised fighting platforms each night.

Even so, an attacker might still try to take the place by a surprise attack. Since Maori *toa* were under no form of discipline beyond their communal responsibilities, strict vigilance on the part of the sentries could only be encouraged, not enforced. If a watchman took time out on a cold night to warm himself by the fire, or dozed at his post, no punishment was due to him. The first recourse of any attacking commander was therefore to assess

An engraving of Maori warriors outside a typical *whare*. *Whares* were retained as living quarters inside a defended position even throughout the New Zealand Wars period. (Author's collection)

the alertness of the enemy sentries at night. Many sentries kept themselves alert by chanting songs; if there was no chanting, and no regular beating of the wooden gong, an attacker might chance a quiet sortie against the gate, hoping to bridge the outer trench and cut away the wooden hurdles before the defenders were alerted by the noise. On one famous occasion an attacking force heard a sentry's chanting die away in the dead of night, and a warrior volunteered to scale the outer palisades. He found the sentry asleep on his tower – killed him quickly and silently jumped down to open the outer gate.

Such easy successes were rare, however. Rather more successful were attempts to capture *pa* by fire. Although the hardwood palisades were difficult to set alight, the *whares* and lighter fences inside were more vulnerable, especially if the defenders had failed to take the precaution of covering them with earth. A difficulty lay, however, in the lack of long-range weapons, and attempts to get close enough to pile up combustible material were usually robustly driven off by the defenders. The usual method of starting a fire in an enemy position was to take a smouldering brand from a campfire, and tie a length of flax to the end. The brand was then whirled around the head until it started to splutter into flame, at which point it was tossed over the palisades. If brands could be thrown high enough to clear the stockade, if they were lucky enough to fall among houses on the other side, and if the defenders were not on hand – or the brands were too many – to put them out, then there was a good chance they might catch on the dry thatch roofs of the *whares*. Many defenders kept a supply of water to hand for just such an eventuality, but once a fire took hold in the inevitably cramped living conditions within it was often

An impressive study of an elderly Maori man wearing a flax cloak decorated with strings and carrying a stone *mere* club. Note the ornate carving on the house behind; such carving was greatly facilitated by the introduction of European metal tools. (Author's collection)

difficult to put out. A favourite time for such an attack was just before dawn on a windy night, when the breeze would fan the flames and the pre-dawn gloom add to the confusion. Once the flames took hold, and as it grew light enough to see, the attacking commander would launch his men in an assault, timed to take advantage of the confusion within.

As practised engineers themselves, the attackers would also search for any weak spots in the defences. Often an attacking commander would instruct his men to build a mound of earth at a safe distance from the enemy *pa*, and from his elevated position upon the summit assess its strengths and weaknesses. A badly constructed angle or unguarded dead ground, approaching close to the palisades, might furnish an opportunity for an attack, if all else failed. Sometimes trenches or saps were dug towards the enemy ramparts in the hope of bringing men close enough to the palisades to be able to start a fire; occasionally the attackers exploited the lie of the ground themselves to dig secret tunnels towards the walls. If not detected, they would attempt to undermine from below the foundations of the palisades, so that these could be pulled down during an assault. In some instances there are references to the defenders having anticipated such a move, and having laid thick creepers across the width of their ramparts during construction, so that the ends lay within the defences. Any attempt at tunnelling was likely to disturb these creepers, a fact which would then be obvious to the defenders.

If an attacking commander felt confident enough to mount an attack his men sometimes advanced under cover of large shields constructed for the purpose, and made of flax laid over a wooden framework. These offered some protection against the defenders' stones and thrown darts, but on the whole the attackers remained acutely vulnerable as they tried to scale trenches and ramparts or clamber over palisades to the spear-thrusts jabbing through the gaps in the stockades, or down from the fighting platforms above. One favourite means of destroying a palisade was an implement known as the *rou*, which was simply a log tied around the middle with a long length of strong creeper. An attacking party would try to get close to a suitable length of palisade and toss the log over the top, pulling back on the rope rather like a European grappling hook. A number of men would then haul on the rope, hoping to drag the palisade down. It was a method that could prove very successful against a stretch of poorly placed, undermined or burnt stockade, but it depended on the success of the attackers in keeping the defenders from cutting the rope.

If an attack successfully reached a palisade, the fighting was often ferocious, despite the physical barriers between the opponents, for the simple reason that survival for both sides depended upon victory. The attackers, in particular, were acutely vulnerable all the time they remained at the palisade – and would be even more so should they turn their backs to flee. Any attacker who fell dead or wounded against a palisade was likely to be dragged within it, particularly if there were gaps at the foot of the palings of the *pekerangi*; the corpse was promptly decapitated by the defenders, and the head carried up and mounted on the palisade to add to the *pa*'s *mana* and discourage the attackers.

If an attacker did manage to force an entry through the outer palisade, the defenders simply retired behind the second line of defences. Here their resistance would be particularly determined, if only because the fate of the entire complex was now at stake. It was quite common for women to join the warriors at this point, lining the tops of the parapets alongside their men and raining stones down upon the attackers. If, however, the attackers managed to break through into a settled area, their chances of success were greatly improved for by setting fire to the *whares* they could make much of the *pa* indefensible. At that point it was time for the defenders to abandon the complex by their planned escape route – if they had one.

Generally, however, direct attacks were only mounted once an attacking commander was convinced that he held some distinct advantage. In most cases, they were not mounted at all, the attacker exhausting every other means of inducing a garrison to surrender, and quite often calling off an attack without ever mounting an assault. Sometimes, indeed, a false withdrawal was a strategy employed to draw the defenders out of the security of their positions, where they would then be ambushed in the open; this was so well known a tactic, however, that defending commanders were usually on their guard for it.

Often an attack on a *pa* would collapse into stalemate. Particularly resolute attackers might choose to invest a *pa*; parties of warriors positioned themselves at key points in the surrounding countryside, built their own shelters from wood and flax, and settled down to wait. It was difficult for attackers to provision themselves indefinitely, however, while the absence of so many men was felt at home. If, on the other hand, the defenders had been able to stock up with a good supply of food and water they were virtually invulnerable behind their stockades. For this reason protracted sieges were rare, although some lasting many months or even a year are recorded in Maori tradition – no doubt precisely because they were exceptional.

If the attackers did pursue a siege long enough, however, there would come a point when the defenders ran out of supplies. Often at that point they would sue for peace – although to be captured condemned the garrison to a life of servitude as slaves of the victors. On some occasions hard-pressed garrisons were forced to resort to cannibalism to survive.

Once a *pa* fell to the enemy it was seldom re-occupied, even if the defences had largely remained in good repair. The *mana* of the site had usually been tainted by defeat, and it was in any case under a *tapu* from the blood of the defenders that had been shed there.

Yet in pre-colonial times the successful capture of a well-sited and well-defended *pa* remained an achievement attained by only the most skilful and determined attacker. Maori fortifications were expertly designed to withstand an array of threats with which the defending engineers were equally familiar. And yet, within the first decades of the 19th century, the introduction of a foreign military technology suddenly rendered obsolete a system of warfare that had endured for hundreds of years.

HONGI HIKA AND THE 'MUSKET WARS'

The publication of Cook's account of New Zealand led to a greater awareness among European mariners of the prevailing conditions in New Zealand and in the years following his visit's the islands became a regular port of call for whalers working the Pacific Ocean and for passing warships and traders seeking a safe haven to repair and reprovision. A small settlement sprang up in the Bay of Islands district, in the north of the North Island, and for the first time Maori and *pakeha* – Europeans – interacted on a regular basis. This interaction was generally encouraged by the *rangatira* of the Ngapuhi *iwi*, who controlled the area, for the trade benefits it brought. A small anarchic settlement sprang up at Kororareka (now Russell) introducing the Maori, among other things, to such Western delights as alcohol, syphilis and gunpowder.

The advantages of the latter, at least, soon became apparent to the Ngapuhi who purchased a small number of flintlock muskets from *pakeha* traders and began experimenting with them in campaigns against rival *iwi*. At the battle of Moremonui in 1808 the Ngapuhi used muskets in battle for the first time against *toa* of the Ngati Whatua *iwi*. It was not an auspicious start; the Ngati Whatua overwhelmed the Ngapuhi while the latter were reloading. The Ngapuhi war-leader was killed together with several of the chiefly line, and the survivors only managed to escape by hiding in a swamp. Among those who survived was Hongi Hika a young *rangatira* who was destined to become chief of the Ngapuhi, and despite this discouraging beginning he became firmly

A section of the palisade of a gunfighters' *pa*, showing the carved figures which adorned the principle posts. In pre-European times the rails and palings were usually lashed on the inside of the posts. (Author's collection)

convinced of the advantages of muskets. As chief he encouraged trade and in 1819 allowed the first Anglican missionary to settle in Ngapuhi territory. As a result of these contacts he was invited by a mission society to visit England and in 1820, after a gruelling voyage as a passenger in a whaler, he spent several months in London and Cambridge. At a time when European knowledge of the world was rapidly expanding, fuelled by an intellectual curiosity and romantic mythologizing of indigenous peoples, Hongi, with his heavily *moko*'d face, created something of a sensation. He was presented to King George IV, and returned to New Zealand laden with gifts. On the way he stopped off in Sydney, sold most of his gifts and purchased 300 muskets and gunpowder.

This gave the Ngapuhi an unquestionable military advantage over neighbouring *iwi*, and on his return Hongi Hika began a series of military campaigns directed at his rivals. His motives remain obscure; he seldom occupied the lands he conquered, and it seems that his aim remained an essentially traditional one – to boost his personal *mana*. The use of firearms on such a scale led to heavy loss of life, particularly in his early campaigns, before his rivals had time to procure muskets of their own. When he overran the *pa* at Tamaki in 1821 the Ngapuhi are said to have killed as many as 2,000 warriors, women and children – an unprecedented loss of life in tribal fighting. Over the next six years Hongi launched a major series of campaigns against the *iwi* in the northern part of the North Island, now known as the 'Musket Wars', dislocating people to an extent seldom experienced in Maori warfare before. Although Hongi's abilities as a general have been questioned, his reliance on muskets generally assured his success.

In January 1827 Hongi Hika was shot through the chest during a minor skirmish – he is said to have called upon those near him to listen to the air whistling through his lungs – and he died as a result of the injury in March 1828.

The Musket Wars spluttered on after his death, exaggerating conflicts within Maori society on the eve of a much greater struggle with Europeans for ownership of New Zealand itself. As many as 20,000 people are said to have died – many of them of course young men in the prime of life – exaggerating a general decline in the Maori population. The fighting led to deep-seated disputes over the validity of tribal boundaries, some of which have not yet been resolved. During subsequent conflicts the British were able to exploit these divisions to the extent that many Maori *iwi* preferred to fight with the *pakeha* in pursuit of long-standing rivalries, and the Maori were never able to provide a united front against European intervention.

Nevertheless, the Musket Wars gave the Maori invaluable experience of firearms, and the changes these had wrought in traditional forms of warfare had generally been recognized, understood and absorbed before the conflicts with the *pakeha* began. The Maori were therefore unusually prepared, for a tribal people, for the unequal struggle which lay ahead of them.

The Musket Wars and the emergence of the 'gunfighters' *pa*'

Late in the 19th century, a Maori warrior left a telling insight into the moment that warfare changed irrevocably in New Zealand:

> We had with us four guns. When we arrived before a *pa*, our marksmen went in front of the party, and as soon as the enemy saw us, they would recognise us as a hostile party, and their warriors would ascend their *puwhara* (fighting stages) so that they might better be able to throw down stones at us. Those

braves did not know of the gun, nor of its deadly effects. When they got up to the platforms, they would grimace and put out their tongues at us. They thought that some of us would be killed by their stones. Whilst they grimaced away, we used to fire at them. It was just like a pigeon falling out of a tree. When the others heard the noise, saw the smoke and the flash, and the death of their braves, they thought it must be the god Maru that accompanied us, and that it was by his power that their men were slain by the thunder of that god Maru. Then the whole *pa* would feel dispirited, and stand without sense, so that we had only to assault the *pa*, without any defence from the people. The people of the *pa* would have all the lamenting and we all the cheers.[6]

As this passage makes clear, it became very apparent early in the Musket Wars that the traditional style of fortified village *pa,* almost impenetrable to an enemy armed only with short-range weapons, had suddenly become obsolete. Men standing on fighting platforms, hitherto a cornerstone of the stockade's defence, were completely exposed to gunfire, against which they had no hope of reply. With the platforms easily cleared, an attacker armed with muskets had little difficulty in mounting an assault directly against the palisading where the gaps left for the spears of the defenders now worked to his advantage. Moreover, where a *pa* was overlooked by nearby rising ground – which had mattered not at all if it were more than a stone's throw away – it was now vulnerable to dropping fire which might rake the interior of the settlement. Moreover anyone venturing out of the *pa*, to fetch water for example, could no longer be defended by men equipped with hand weapons alone.

These realities led to a shift in Maori military engineering away from the methods that had protected their settlements for centuries towards a new style of fortification specifically intended for use in the age of gunpowder – the so-called 'gunfighters' *pa*'.

One early manifestation of this was a shift away from hilltops as an ideal site for a *pa* and towards sites on gently sloping or level ground. Such sites could be built closer to cultivated land, usually commanded a good field of fire, were seldom overlooked and removed both something of the hard physical labour of dragging logs, supplies and water up a steep slope and the subsequent risk to the occupants of descending during a siege to the nearest source of water. Also, it was quickly perceived that it was no longer necessary to build so many and such deep trenches, or so many rows of stockades. The third and fourth lines of palisade became largely superfluous, and most gunfighters' *pa* had only two – the *pekerangi,* or outer screen, and a main inner stockade. Nor was it necessary to have such high palisades, constructed

A reconstructed *pa* from the Christchurch Exhibition of 1906. Although this includes splendid fighting stages, the palisades are of the smaller post-firearms type.

6 Quoted in Best, *The Pa Maori.*

of such great logs. The favourite *puriri* wood of old remained ideally suited to the new style of defence in that it was extremely hard and impenetrable to musket bullets; Elsdon Best, that great early 20th-century expert on Maori culture, noted that he had examined a number of posts from a *pa* attacked by British troops in the 1860s. They still contained many Enfield bullets that had passed through the dry outer layers but had flattened out on the tough sap-wood within. Nevertheless the support posts for the palisades of most gunfighters' *pa* were noticeable shorter than had previously been common.

There were changes too in the number and size of the ramparts. Since it soon became impractical to stand on the top of high banks as in the old days, earthworks were constructed with a view to concealing and sheltering defenders armed themselves with muskets. For the first time *banquettes* or firing steps were constructed to enable defenders to fire over ramparts. Trenches were usually dug inside the lines of palisades, so that the defenders could kneel or lie in them, firing through the stockade. To facilitate their fire, not all of the palings between the support posts extended to the ground, the short ones leaving gaps at the bottom to act as loopholes for the defenders in the trenches behind. Further trenches were often dug to facilitate communication between areas of the *pa*, so that defenders moving about within could so without being exposed to enemy fire. The palings and their supporting rails were increasingly fixed to the outside of a palisade – rather than the inside – to further delay an attacker at close range while mats of green flax were draped over the outer palisades to deaden the shot.

The *pekerangi*, indeed, came to be regarded increasingly not just as a barricade but as a screen to hold up an attack in place within easy range of men concealed behind the main stockade beyond. It became common practise for Maori defenders to hold their fire until their enemy was just 40 or 50m away, and then deliver a devastating volley from behind the *pekerangi*. If the assault continued, the men in the forward trenches would fall back, leaving the attackers exposed – rather as men trying to penetrate the wire screens before trenches were in World War I – to fire from the main stockade as they struggled to break through the *pekerangi*.

The shape of the new *pa* also reflected their purpose. No longer following the essentially circular contours of a hill, they were often variations on a square or rectangle, so as to present concentrated fields of fire against the enemy on all sides. To protect the angles, projecting bastions were often built at one or more corner to provide flanking fire down the face of each side. One account refers to trenches within the *pa* being built with traverses between them at intervals of every few metres, the purpose apparently being to limit the view of the men using them on either side, in case they became discouraged by the sight of casualties further down the line!

Another new feature of musket warfare was the use of rifle pits. These were simple trenches, dug deep enough to shelter a crouching man – sometimes

A sketch of the entrance to a *pa* in the 1860s. It was not unusual for the gateway to be cut through a single tree-trunk, which was then highly decorated. (Author's collection)

deeper – with the earth thrown up in front to form a parapet. They were constructed on the approaches to a *pa* so as to exploit the ground, commanding ground that was otherwise sheltered from the defenders' fire and funnelling attacks along predictable courses. Usually such pits were positioned with escape routes in mind – with a clear field of fire in front and bush behind – to enable the defenders to slip away as the enemy approached, perhaps to join the main body in the *pa*.

The principles of the gunfighters' *pa* were established during the conflicts of the 1820s, and were in almost universal usage by the time the wars against Europeans began in the 1840s. As successive British commanders were to discover, they were ideally suited to counter the conventional European tactics of the day – and they would evolve still further as the Maori found themselves increasingly on the receiving end of artillery fire.

THE 'NEW ZEALAND WARS'

In the first decades of the 19th century, while the Maori of the North Island were occupied with the Musket Wars, the European population of New Zealand expanded rapidly. The impetus was largely commercial. European empires were expanding around the world as the Napoleonic Wars drew to a close, and the hinterland of the Bay of Islands offered not only a chance for passing ships to stock up on food but commodities which were themselves in demand, like flax and timber. While many of the northern Maori groups, such as Hongi Hika's Ngapuhi, enjoyed the advantages of trading with the *pakeha*, not least for guns, others became concerned at the rapid and un-policed expansion of European settlements. This included the British authorities who, because of their interests in Australia, considered New Zealand to be within their sphere of influence, and were worried by both French and American involvement there. The British therefore established a resident to represent their interests in the Islands but, concerned that he lacked authority over the settlers and had no legal influence over the independent Maori, the British Government despatched Captain William Hobson, Royal Navy, to reach an agreement with the Maori which would recognize a broader British claim to the islands. Hobson drafted a treaty – known as the Treaty of Waitangi – which he presented to many of the northern chiefs at Kororareka in the first week of

British troops outside the palisades of the Makahi-Nuku *pa* during the Hutt Valley campaign of 1847. (Author's collection)

February 1840. Initially the treaty was signed by the influential *ariki* of the Ngapuhi, Hone Heke – a nephew of the great Hongi Hika – and 45 of his fellow chiefs, and over the following weeks many more *rangatira* added their signatures. It was generally recognized that the treaty allowed for the establishment of a British governor in New Zealand and guaranteed the rights of the Maori to their lands, which could only to be sold to settlers through the intervention of the British Crown. Beyond that, however, it seems that both parties had different understandings of the agreement, and

Pricipal *pa* sites and areas of Maori resistance

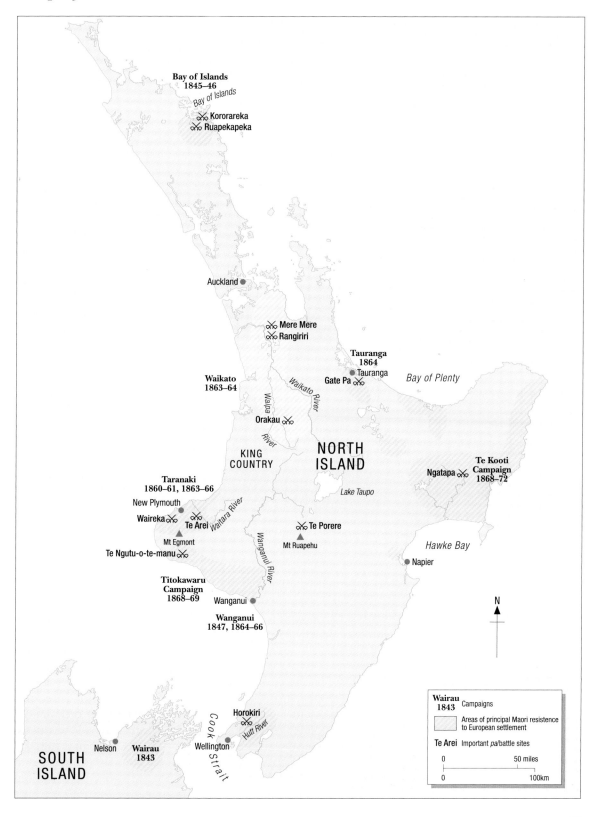

Bay of Islands
1845–46

Bay of Islands

Kororareka
Ruapekapeka

Auckland

Mere Mere
Rangiriri

Waikato
1863–64

Tauranga
1864

Tauranga

Gate Pa

Bay of Plenty

Waikato River

Waipa

Orakau

River

KING
COUNTRY

NORTH
ISLAND

Te Kooti
Campaign
1868–72

Ngatapa

Taranaki
1860–61, 1863–66

New Plymouth

Waireka

Te Arei

Lake Taupo

Waitara River

Mt Egmont

Te Ngutu-o-te-manu

Te Porere

Mt Ruapehu

Hawke Bay

Napier

Wanganui River

Titokawaru
Campaign
1868–69

Wanganui

Wanganui
1847, 1864–66

N

Horokiri

Hutt River

Cook Strait

Nelson

Wairau
1843

Wellington

SOUTH
ISLAND

Wairau
1843 Campaigns

Areas of principal Maori resistence
to European settlement

Te Arei Important *pa*/battle sites

0   50 miles

0   100km

the question of land ownership had only recently been complicated by the recent Musket Wars. In fact, friction between Maori and *pakeha* steadily increased after the signing of the treaty; white settlers argued that it gave them Crown protection in their attempts to prise land from the Maori while the Maori thought precisely the opposite. The terms and conditions of the Treaty of Waitangi, and the implications since, are still the subject of debate and legal claims today.

Once again land provided the impetus for conflict as New Zealand steadily filled over the following decades with European immigrants. Although each outbreak had a specific cause and flash point, the steady increase in European demand for land, and a refusal of the Maori to countenance it, was the consistent underlying cause of a cycle of wars that began in the 1840s and did not finally end until the 1870s. Each was essentially a local conflict as successive *iwi* and *hapu* came under pressure in turn. Although some Maori groups formed temporary alliances – and a 'king movement', which offered a Maori king as a counter to the British queen emerged in the 1850s – they never achieved a united front in defence of their land. In times of open conflict British troops were almost always supported by Maori who were either pursuing independent policies or were locked in older conflicts with the groups attacked by the British.

The first clash – untypically – took place at Wairau, at the northern tip of the South Island, in 1843. Here a settlement had been established at Nelson in 1841 but their hope of expanding into the territory of the Ngati Toa *iwi* met with firm resistance. The Ngati Toa turned away British surveyors and when these persisted the Maori burned down their huts. Angry settlers from Nelson set off on 13 June to arrest the Ngati Toa *ariki* Te Ruaparaha. After an angry confrontation with the chief and his followers on the banks of the Tuamarina stream a scuffle broke out and shots were fired. Both settlers and Maori were killed, and while some settlers fled another group surrendered. When it transpired that Te Ruaparaha's daughter had been killed, however, the Maori claimed *utu* – and 12 settlers were promptly cut down by tomahawk.

It was the first of a good deal of blood destined to be shed between the Maori and *pakeha*. Ironically, the Governor refused to support the settler position, recognizing that they had acted impetuously, but almost immediately there was a further outbreak at the far end of the islands. Although the Ngapuhi Chief Hone Heke, in the Bay of Islands area, had been the first signatory of the Treaty of Waitangi, it soon became apparent that the establishment of a new British administrative centre at Auckland deprived his people of many of the trade advantages they had enjoyed when Kororareka had been the principle European settlement. Heke vented his frustration by cutting down the flagpole from which the British flag flew on a prominent hill over Kororareka. The British put it back up; twice more Hone cut it down until, after a fourth time, he led his warriors in an attack on the settlement. The settlers took refuge in ships at anchor in the harbour while the Ngapuhi burned their houses. As soon as the news reached Auckland, British troops were hurried to the Bay of Islands area.

The subsequent campaign established a pattern that was to be repeated, with variations, over and over again during the next 30 years. Heke and his ally, the Ngatihine chief Kawiti, built a number of *pa*; the British attacked them using conventional tactics, usually opening with a preliminary artillery bombardment then mounting a direct assault. These assaults were usually driven off before the Maori, having achieved their objectives, abandoned their *pa*. In the end a decisive element in the conflict was provided by Heke's rivalry with a powerful war-chief of his own tribe, Tamati Waka Nene, who had objected to the attack on Kororareka. Nene allied himself to the British, and it was fighting between his followers and Heke – rather than the efforts of British troops – which persuaded Heke and Kawiti to negotiate and brought the war to a close in early 1846.

Trouble flared almost immediately in the south of North Island, however. The Ngati Toa *iwi* occupied land on both sides of the Cook Straight, and Te Ruaparaha – involved in the

British troops storming a *pa*. Although this illustration represents a battle in the 1860s, it is in fact far more typical of the fighting of the 1840s. (Author's collection)

Wairau Incident on the South Island – had retired to tribal lands on North Island. In the early 1840s settler interests had purchased land in the Hutt Valley from representatives of a *hapu* driven out by the Ngati Toa during the Musket Wars. Although these Maori had a good claim to the land it was the Ngati Toa who actually occupied it. When settlers arrived to mark out farms in the Hutt Valley the Ngati Toa resisted. In February 1846 British troops tried to clear the Hutt of Maori settlements and this provoked Maori attacks in turn on the settlers. On 16 May a British outpost at Boulcott's Farm was attacked for several hours before the Maori were driven off. Although Te Ruaparaha had played no active part in the fighting he was captured by the British and sent to Auckland. A *pa* built by his nephew Te Rangihaeata – who had played a prominent part in the Wairau affair – at Horokiri was bombarded by British troops until the Maori abandoned it. Although the Maori had not been significantly defeated in the field they chose to end the conflict by abandoning the Hutt Valley to white settlement. Many Maori retired to the Wanganui district, where a small European settlement had been established in 1841, and over the following months tension in that area grew, breaking out into desultory and inconclusive fighting in 1847.

The fighting of the 1840s had resolved little beyond underscoring the underlying competition between European settlers and the Maori for land. Over the next 20 years the situation was further exacerbated by a large influx of British settlers, to the extent that by 1859 it has been estimated that Maori and *pakeha* population levels had achieved parity at about 60,000 each. With the Maori still owning title to most of the land, but effectively utilizing only a fraction of it, and with European settlements unable to contain the expansionist ambitions of frustrated settlers, the stage was set for further conflict. The British were, moreover, increasingly inclined to resolve disputes by extending British authority across hitherto independent areas. In March 1859 settlers were offered for sale of block of land at Waitara, in the Taranaki district on the west coast of the North Island. They enthusiastically agreed, despite the fact that it became clear that the offer had been made with the express opposition of senior Maori chiefs. The British Governor accepted the sale, however, and moved troops into the Waikato to support the settler claims. The result was a campaign that lasted for a year from March 1860 during which the fighting largely followed the pattern established in earlier

wars. The Maori would build a *pa*, either with a specific strategic intent – to threaten survey parties, British camps or important roads – or simply in the hope of provoking a decisive engagement. For the most part the British were unable to evict the Maori from their positions by force. The decisive fighting took place around the *pa* of Te Arei in January 1861. Here the British commander, General Pratt, attempted to take the Maori positions by sapping – digging a long trench towards the enemy to protect the advance of his men. It took ten weeks to reach the outskirts of the *pa*, at which point the Maori agreed to a negotiated peace settlement. Although the British occupied the disputed Waitara block, many disaffected Maori simply moved elsewhere and the fundamental issues behind the conflict were again not resolved.

In 1861 one of the most dynamic British administrators to serve in New Zealand, Sir George Grey, returned to the islands for a second term as governor, and the simmering discontent entered a new phase. Grey was concerned to reduce Maori resistance to settler expansionism, and in particular recognized the 'king movement' as a dangerous focus of emergent Maori nationalism. The 'king movement' had its heartland in the Waikato, north of Taranaki, and when the resentments still smouldering in the Taranaki again flared into violence in 1863, Grey saw the Waikato chiefs as the instigators of it. In July 1863 Grey's troops crossed the border into kingite Waikato territory. The invasion of the Waikato was to prove the largest conflict yet, employing thousands of British troops, allied Maori and settler militia; throughout the wars, it is unlikely, however, that Maori forces ever numbered more than 5,000, of whom no more than 2,000 were involved in any single conflict.

The fighting began cautiously with the British commander, General Cameron, pushing forwards tentatively and constructing a string of outposts to protect his lines of communication. These the Maori harassed, and for arguably the first time in the wars they built lines of entrenchments with the specific strategic intention of blocking the British advance. The Maori had built a strong position at Mere Mere but Cameron bypassed it by sending steamers, loaded with troops, up the Waikato River. The Maori repeated the same tactic at Rangiriri, which Cameron attacked on 20 November. The British failed to capture the position but the following morning, in circumstances that are still contested, the Maori surrendered. Cameron pressed on, bypassing another chain of defences at Paterangi, and the last major action of the campaign took place at chief Rewi Maniapoto's *pa* at Orakau in March 1864. In an incident that came to symbolize Maori defiance, Rewi repulsed a succession of British assaults before enduring three days of siege, much of it without water. At the end of this, refusing British requests to surrender, some 250 Maori made a sudden and successful dash for freedom through the British lines.

Although the Maori had built further lines to contest the British advance, Governor Grey decided that enough of the Waikato had been occupied and hostilities came to a close. Grey followed his successes by authorizing the confiscation of thousands of square kilometres of Maori land, confirming in Maori minds the link between settler ambitions and military policy. This encouraged the support of further resistance movements, notably the emergence of the Pai Marire religion, which fused Christian and traditional Maori beliefs – including the revival of ceremonial cannibalism – and which was committed to the preservation of Maori culture and to the retention of land. Adherents of the Pai Marire were known to the settlers as 'Hau Hau' from the chants accompanying their battlefield rituals.

The result was a series of further outbreaks that dragged on through the 1860s in Taranaki, again, and in Tauranga, on the east coast, where Maori *iwi* had been vociferous in defence of their neighbours in the Waikato. Much of this fighting was waged on the European side by settler militia and by allied Maori groups as the regular British Army sought from 1865 to extricate themselves from the entanglement. Although the fighting remained regional until 1868 the increased willingness of European forces to used 'scorched-earth' tactics, driving Maori out of contested areas, the attrition inflicted on the non-professional Maori forces and the process of confiscation of Maori land meant that by 1868 the fighting had dissolved into sporadic acts of guerrilla warfare. In particular, the Nga Ruahinerangi *rangatira* Titokawaru waged a very successful campaign from his stronghold at Te Ngutu o te Manu in the south west while a commoner, Te Kooti Arikirangi, emerged as a daring and ruthless guerrilla leader on the east coast. Although Titokawaru's support among his followers declined – apparently as a result of a loss of *mana* following his adultery with the wife of another chief – neither he nor Te Kooti were captured.

B

Ruapekapeka

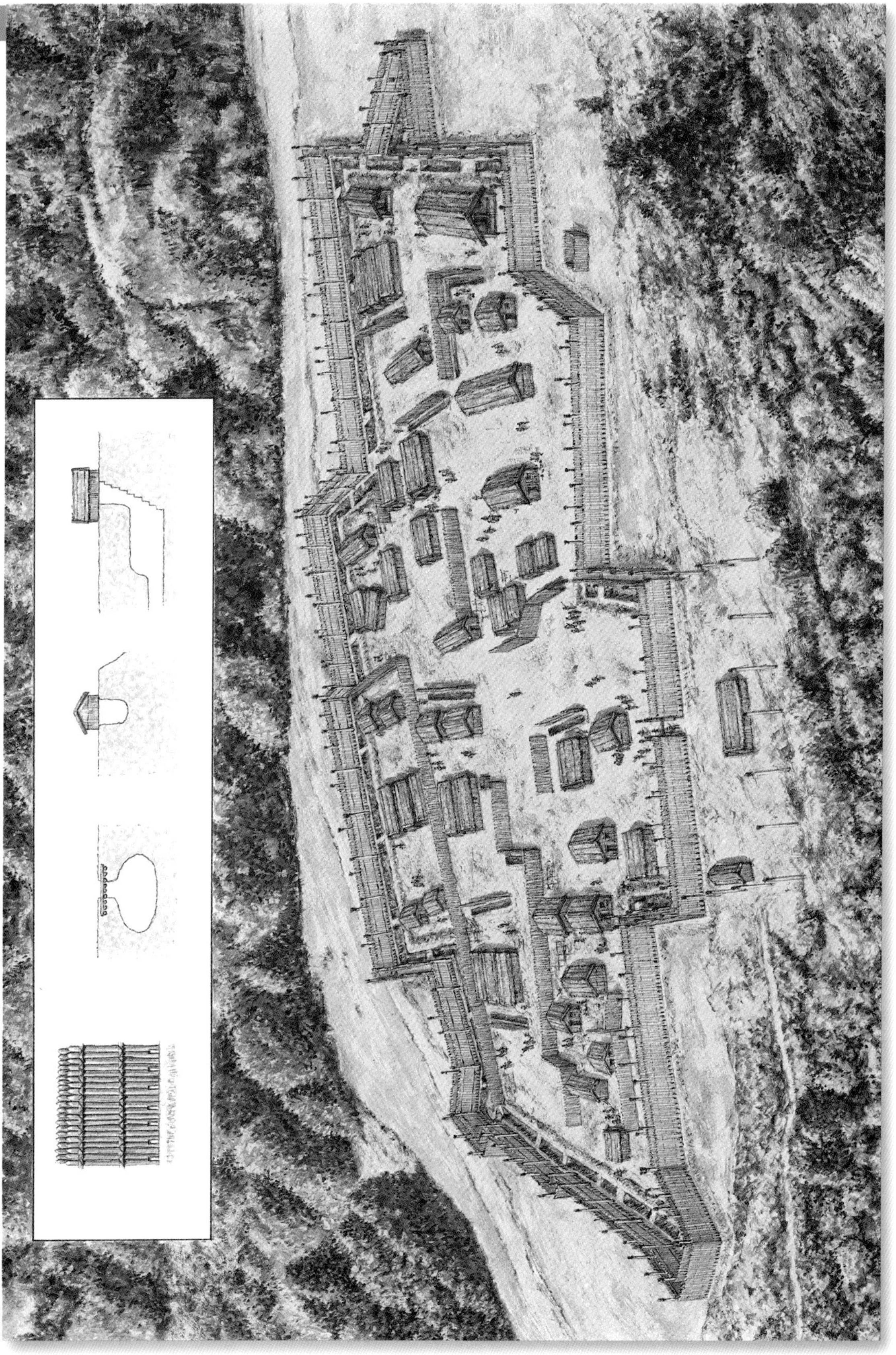

British troops attacking Kawiti's Ruapekepeka *pa* in January 1846 – a picture that stresses the formidable nature of the outer palisades. (Michael Graham-Stewart)

Harried by colonial forces, they were eventually reduced to a handful of followers and both chose to retire to inaccessible areas rather than surrender.

By 1872 armed resistance among the Maori to the occupation of their land had ceased, but other forms of protest would continue. In 1880 a large number of Taranaki Maori established a settlement at Parihaka with the intention of living beyond the reach of colonial authority; in 1881 troops occupied Parihaka in what might have been the last action of the wars, had the Maori leadership opted for passive rather than active resistance.

The *pa* in the 1840s

In the aftermath of the Musket Wars the Maori were ideally placed to confront the British with the recently perfected concepts embodied in the gunfighters' *pa*. These only required further modification to make them equally resistant to British artillery fire. Mats – and sometimes stuffed woven sacks – were used to deaden the effect of the shells while the palings in the palisades were increasing tied on individually rather than by a common rope in sections. This meant that if a shell struck one piece of the palisade it would not tear down whole sections and the damage was limited to those pales and

An aerial photograph of Ruapekepeka, one of the best-preserved *pa* sites from the New Zealand Wars period. The profile of the outer defences can clearly be seen here, complete with the traces of internal shelters and rifle pits. (Kevin L Jones/New Zealand Department of Conservation)

posts actually struck. It also reduced the risk of splinters of wood being scattered in among the defenders by an explosion. Even in the 1840s Maori engineers learned to dig deep underground pits within a *pa* to shelter the defenders; where non-combatants were living in a stockade with their men, such shelters were often dug under the *whares* to shelter the occupants during an attack. Often rifle pits and front-line trenches were roofed over with wood and piled with earth.

That these principles were readily understood from the start of the conflicts with the British is evident from a description by Major Cyprian Bridge of the 58th Regiment of Hone Heke's Puketutu *pa* in May 1845:

> The *pa* was built on a slight eminence, was square in shape, but zigzagged at the corners in order to bring a crossfire to bear on its assailants. It had three rows of tree-trunk palisades, 15 feet in height, sunk to several feet in the ground, each tree-trunk 5 to 6 inches in diameter, set close together. A mass of stone rubble, collected from the volcanic debris scattered about, further strengthened the foundations of the *pekerangi* (or outer fence). The palisading was carefully caulked with green flax to prevent enemy bullets penetrating the apertures; loopholes were everywhere prepared to facilitate the defence, and to render its storming still more difficult, a deep trench was dug between the deep wooden walls.[7]

Similar features were noted in a report by Major Last, 99th Regiment, of Te Rangihaeta's *pa* at Matai-taua during the Hutt Valley campaign, a complex which apparently reflected a transitional stage as the Maori were just beginning to appreciate the dangers posed by artillery:

> On examining the *pa*, I found it built on a very strong position, having a double row of timber palisades, with trenches and traverses across, about 80 paces long, and 35 broad, in the shape of a parallelogram with flanking defences.

7 Major Cyprian Bridge, *Journal of Events on an Expedition to New Zealand*, quoted in Ryan and Parham, *The Colonial New Zealand Wars*, Wellington, 1986.

Ruapekapeka again, showing how the *pa* was built on a commanding rise. The British established a camp along the (modern) road towards the top right of the picture from which to invest and attack Ruapekepeka.
(Kevin L Jones/New Zealand Department of Conservation)

There was also a bank of earth thrown up on the scarp side of the trenches, which, owing to the heavy rain, were full of water. The position altogether is a very strong one, and would have been almost impregnable without artillery, but a hill about 500 yards distant opposite the front face commanded it completely. … The *pa* stands on a very high ground fronting the harbour; at the foot of it runs a deep narrow creek, fordable at low water; the ground about is excessively swampy, which the troops had to pass over. On the side the *pa* stands rises a very steep bank, which, even without opposition, the men had difficulty in climbing. And on the proper left of the position is a very deep ravine, the side of which is thickly wooded. The right face is also thickly wooded, and the ground gradually slopes away into a valley. The rear was the weakest part as to its defence, the ground covered with thick scrub, but from its position I do not consider a position could have been taken up by us on that side.[8]

Hone Heke's *pa* of Ohaeawai, in the Bay of Islands district, proved to be even more impressive:

The inside fence was made of a very hard wood which does not splitter much; the posts of this fence were about one fathom in the ground and the fence over

8 Report by Major Last, 99th Regiment, dated 4 August 1846.

A photo of a late-period *pa* with a light outer palisade.
(Author's collection)

A sketch by Major Cyprian Bridge of the 58th Regiment depicting an attack on a *pa* in May 1845. The main Maori fortifications are to the left, although a line of palisades has been extended to include an abandoned European building, right. (Alexander Turnbull Library, National Library of New Zealand)

ground was about four fathoms high. The posts were stout, and some of them would require thirty men with ropes to raise them. Inside this fence was the trench in which men stood to fire; their faces only reached the level of the ground outside the fort. The loopholes, though which the men fired, were also only level with the ground outside, so that in firing the men were very slightly exposed, Outside of all was the *pekerangi*, which is a lighter sort of fence put up to deaden the force of shot before it strikes the inner one, and also intended to delay a storming party, so that while they would be pulling it down, the men behind the inner fence might have time to shoot them. This *pekerangi* was nearly as high as the inner fence, and stood little more than half a fathom outside of it; it was made of a strong framework, and was padded thickly with green flax to deaden the force of shot. It was also elevated about a foot from the ground, so that the men behind the inner fence, standing in the ditch, could shoot through the loopholes in the inner fence and under the outside fence; also at different distances along the *kauae* (curtain) there were *koki* (fighting angles), capable of containing many men, so that the storming party would be exposed to a fire both in front and flank, and in these angles were put large ship guns. The men inside, in the inner trench, were also protected from flanking parties by *pakiaka* (traverses), which crossed the trench at intervals; also inside the place were many excavations underground covered over with large logs or timber, and over the timber earth. In these pit's the men could sleep safe from the shot of the big guns of the soldiers. There were also high platforms at the corners of the inner fence, from whence could be seen all that the enemy might be doing outside.[9]

9 F. E. Maning, *Old New Zealand*, Auckland 1863.

The defences of Ohaeawai were to prove as formidable as they looked, for they withstood one of the few determined frontal assaults made upon Maori entrenchments in the course of the fighting.

Perhaps the most impressive complex built during the wars of the 1840s, and one which has deservedly remained famous as a classic example of Maori engineering skills, was Kawiti's *pa* at Ruapekapeka, described with considerable professional appreciation by the man who attacked it, Colonel Henry Despard;

The *pa* itself was an oblong square, with projecting works on each face, and at two of the angles, so as to form a flanking fire in every direction. The first range of stockade was about 10 ft high, composed of either whole trees of the *puriri* wood, the hardest and toughest wood known in New Zealand, or of split timbers of the same wood, sunk in the ground from 2 ft to 3 ft deep, and placed close to each other. Many of the former were from 12 in. to 15 in. in diameter, and loopholed close to the ground. Within this stockade on two faces, at 3 ft distance, was another stockade, equally strong, also loopholed close to the ground, corresponding with those in front; and within that again was a ditch 5 ft deep, and the same breadth, with an embankment of earth on the inner side, behind which a man could lie and fire through the loopholes of both fences. On the other faces the ditch was between the two stockade fences. The ditch was divided, at every 5 ft or 6ft, by traverses, leaving a small opening passage, not opposite each other, but alternate on either side. The ground in the interior was excavated in many places to afford shelter to the garrison

A sketch by Major Cyprian Bridge of British troops firing on Hone Heke's Ohaiawai *pa* in June 1845. The British have screened their positions behind a rampart and palisade; the extent of the outer Maori palisade is very obvious, as are the loopholes at ground level. (Alexander Turnbull Library, National Library of New Zealand)

from cannon shot. Some of these excavations were entered from the ditch, and others were thatched over to keep out the wet.[10]

Typically Ruapekapeka was built in a commanding position, on the forward slope of a hill that dominated the approach routes, with ground falling away steeply on two sides. It was also surrounded by bush, which both hampered the enemy and provided the defenders with cover when operating outside the *pa*, as well as with an escape route.

The *pa* of the 1860s

The campaigns of the 1840s convinced the Maori that the ability to resist artillery fire was an essential requirement of *pa* design. The fighting of the 1860s was, of course, widespread, involving many different chiefs and *hapu*, and, as in pre-colonial times, individuals designed and built their *pa* according to their military objectives and to the lie of the land. While in many cases *pa* were built to issue a specific challenge to British troops, and to invite a decisive contest, during the Waikato campaign they were increasingly built as a physical barrier to the British advance. Sometimes they were built on flat ground, or on slight rises in the open, flanked by natural features that channelled enemy attacks along predictable lines. Generally, the use of stockades declined across the period, with entrenchments and underground shelters assuming greater prominence as the main form of defence. Sometimes just the *pekerangi* was constructed, not for protection but to provide an obstacle to pin the enemy in place at a point when he could best be exposed to the defenders' fire. Sometimes the complexity of the entrenchments served not only to protect the defenders but as a means in themselves of confusing the enemy assault. An increasingly common feature was the use of outlying rifle pits, built some way in advance of the main works, and often protected by wooden roofing and difficult to spot.

Yet even these trends were subject to considerable variation – Titokawaru's *pa* at Tauranga-Ika, built as late as 1869, was widely acknowledged as a superb

10 Despard, quoted in Ryan and Parham, *The Colonial New Zealand Wars*.

The British attack on Orakau at the beginning of April 1864. British troops had assembled at a peach grove, right, and then advanced towards the *pa* by means of a sap. (Author's collection)

example of the art of construction, and included both bombproof dwellings and a double line of palisades. Often, *pa* could be erected in a remarkably short time, and parties of 200 or 300 men could construct a fortification in 48 hours or less, a process aided by Maori access to metal European tools such as saws, picks and shovels.

A detailed description of the Taranaki *pa* at Manutahi suggests the extent to which Maori engineers had profited by earlier exposure to artillery:

> The front palisading reached across from bush to bush, perhaps 100 to 120 feet in length, the ends being carried well into the bush and blocked and screened with branches and native briar. The supports of the front palisade (as also the others) were of tree boles about twelve inches in diameter, sunk deeply and firmly into the ground about ten feet apart and projecting above the ground to a height of 12 to 14 feet. To these were lashed horizontally, with supple jack and rata-vine, at heights of about 3 feet 6 inches and 10 feet from the ground, heavy split rails … and to these, vertically and fairly close together, were lashed other split rails, the tops about the height of the posts, and the butts reaching to about 1 foot above the ground. Behind this palisading was a trench 8 feet deep by 10 feet wide at the top and 6 feet wide at the bottom; behind this again was a second palisade similar in design and strength to the front one. Behind this, firing galleries or passages had been dug parallel with the front. The galleries were about 5 feet deep by 3 feet wide – not dug in one straight line, but with blocks or traverses about every 20 feet to provide against the effect of a bursting shell. These galleries were roofed over with logs on which were placed saplings and fern, well trampled down. The whole was covered with the earth from the trenches and galleries; this covering was from 3 to 4 feet deep. The front galleries or firing trenches extended the full length of the *pa*. Loopholes were left under the log covering (about on a level with the outer front) through which the Maoris could fire on the advancing foe without themselves being seen or being in danger. From the firing galleries passages went back to a central passage in the *pa* (covered in the same manner as the others), which in turn led by a covered way to the gully and stream in the bush, by which passage the Maoris could escape in case of defeat, or could be reinforced during the fighting. The sides and rear of the pa had single palisading only, inside the trench, as the Maoris did not expect any assault on those sides. In front of the *pa* for a distance of about 300 yards all fern had been broken down or removed; so for that distance no cover was afforded the advancing enemy and the defenders could see them and fire at them from the loopholes. … The heaviest field-gun used by the troops at that time was the 24 lb howitzer, throwing solid shot or shell. Either of these striking the vertical palisading would simply cut the piece struck, and, as it was tied in three places, the ends would swing back again, leaving the palisade apparently as before. Should a shot strike a post it might smash it down, but rarely did so. (At Puke-at-kauere in 1860 I saw the artillery, at 300 yards and under, fire at the palisading for over an hour without doing any appreciable damage.) … The chances were more than a hundred to one against a ball or shell entering a loophole through which the Maoris fired. … Assuming the outer palisade was broken down, the assaulting party would have to face the trench and inner palisade, and were these overcome and the enemy got into the *pa*, they would see nothing but a bare earth surface. The Maoris could not be got at, but would escape by a covered way into the gully or bush, where they could not be followed.[11]

11 Account by a settler, George Robinson, quoted in James Cowan, *The New Zealand Wars*.

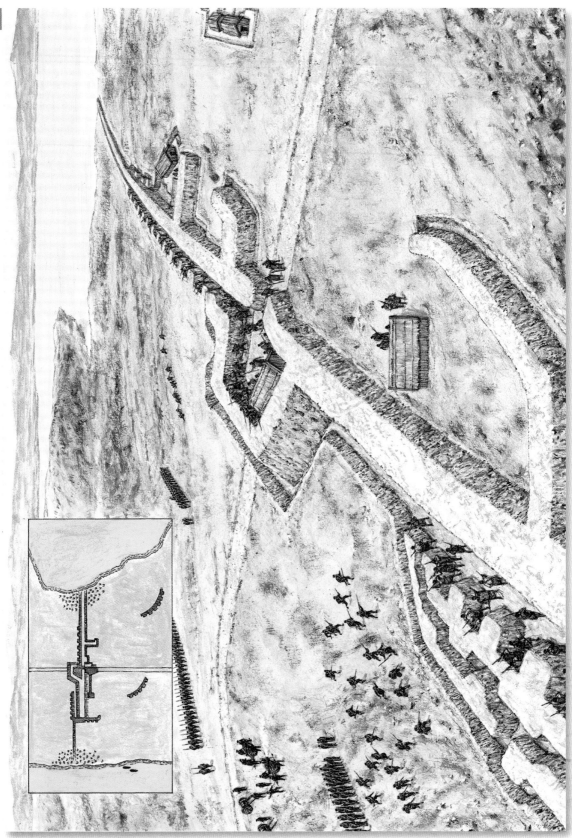

During the Waikato campaign the Maori built extensive lines of earthworks – redoubts linked by trenches – at Mere Mere and Rangiriri to halt the British advance. In these the traditional use of palisades was abandoned altogether. At Rangiriri, according to Major-General Alexander, the Maori position had been well chosen and lay on a slight rise on a narrow strip of land lying between two stretches of water:

> The enemy's works consisted of a line of high parapet and double ditch, extending between the Waikato River and Lake Waikare, the centre of this line being strengthened by a square redoubt of very considerable construction, its ditch being 12 ft wide, and the height from the bottom of the ditch to the top of the parapet 18 ft. The strength of this work was not known before the attack, as its profile could not be seen from the river or from the ground in front. Behind the centre of this main line, and at right angles to it, there was a strong interior line of rifle pits facing the river, and obstructing the advance of the troops from that direction. About 500 yards behind the front of the position was a high ridge, the summit of which was fortified by rifle pits.[12]

12 Maj. Gen. Alexander, quoted in Ryan and Parham, *The Colonial New Zealand Wars*.

The attack on the Okaihou *pa* on 8 May 1845. A firing line of men in skirmishing order engage the *pa* in the middle distance, with their supports lined up in reserve, next to them are friendly Maori. Although smoke emerging from the base of the stockade indicates that resistance was continuing, some of the defenders are escaping from the rear of the *pa*. (Alexander Turnbull Library, National Library of New Zealand)

C RANGIRIRI

Rangiriri was a complex earthwork built on a narrow strip of land lying between the Waikato River and Lake Waikare; it was attacked by the British in November 1863. The design of the *pa* reflected a further shift away from pre-colonial models in that it abandoned wooden palisades entirely, relying instead on a series of inter-connected and deeply entrenched redoubts. The *pa* was built in an exposed position that afforded the British little cover, and the approaches were further screened by rifle pits. British troops under General Cameron were landed from gunboats on the Waikato River and assaulted the position on 20 November 1863. Although some outlying defences were successfully stormed the attacks bogged down in the deep trenches surrounding the main redoubts. The British troops remained in their positions overnight, however, and when the Maori raised a white flag on the morning of the 21st in the hope of opening negotiations the British assumed they were surrendering and in the confusion occupied the *pa*. Two British officers and 35 men were killed in the attack and 93 men wounded, and of these four officers and six men later died of their injuries. The Maori lost 45 dead and 183 captured. The battle for Rangiriri proved to be a decisive British victory in the capture of the Waikato.

Pukehinahina, the famous Gate *pa* in Tauranga – so called because it had been constructed close to a gate in a fence separating Maori and mission land – also consisted of a long trench built over a commanding rise and reinforced with one extensive and one small redoubt. It was screened only by a light *pekerangi* palisade. At Moturoa in November 1868 the Pai Marire adherents built a long angled trench across a clearing in the bush, securing the centre and flanks with redoubts and placing only a single palisade across the front.

At Tauranga-Ika, however, Titokawaru constructed an impressive complex that melded the best of both modern and traditional construction techniques:

> It was of large size, fully defended with palisading, trenches, parapet and rifle pits. It was between two and three chains in extreme length at the rear, with a somewhat narrower front. ... The two rows of palisades, high and strong, were erected around the position; the posts, solid tree trunks between the larger stockade posts were filled in with saplings set upright close together, and fastened by cross-rails and supple jack ties; these saplings did not rest on the ground, but hung a few inches above it, so that between them and the ground a space was left for the fire of the defending musketeers, who were enabled to pour volleys from their trenches behind the war fence on any approaching enemy with perfect safety to themselves. Behind the inner stockading was a parapet about 6ft high and 4ft wide, formed of the earth thrown out of the trenches. The interior of the *pa* was pitted everywhere with trenches and covered ways, so that in the event of an attack, the defenders could literally take to the earth like rabbits, and live underground secure from rifle fire, and even from artillery. The place was a network of trenches with connecting passages, roofed over with timber, *raupo*, reeds and earth. To any assault that could be delivered by the Government forces then available, the fort was practically impregnable.
>
> At one angle of the *pa* the Hahau garrison erected a roughly timbered watchtower about 35ft in height ... there were two gateways in the rear stockading, giving access to the bush.[13]

13 Account of Kimble Bent, a British deserter who joined the Maori, quoted in Cowan, *The New Zealand Wars*.

Maori defences at Mere Mere on the Waikato River were built to prevent British troops passing up the river; too formidable to risk a frontal assault, the British commander, General Cameron, bypassed them in October 1863 with the use of gunboats. (Author's collection)

The British response to the *pa*

Across 30 years of intermittent warfare British troops were faced with not only the physical difficulties of overcoming successive *pa*, but also a persistent conundrum. The gunfighters' *pa* of the New Zealand Wars differed from a traditional fortified village not only by its design, but also in intent. Most of the old pre-colonial *pa* were permanent fortified villages, built to protect their inhabitants for so long as they lived in the area. Although the British certainly attacked some long-standing settlements – such as Chief Pomare's *pa* at Otuihu at the beginning of the Northern War – most *pa* built during struggles against Europeans were not intended as settlements but were intended as a short-term military challenge. They were built to threaten existing British positions or lines of communications, to block a British advance or simply, as often or not, as an act of defiance. Many *pa* were built with the express intention of tempting the British to attack them in the hope of winning local military advantage or simply boosting the *mana* of the defenders.

The British initially approached *pa* with a conventional European outlook. They saw them as strongholds that encouraged and supported Maori resistance, and they assumed that by capturing them they would deal a significant blow to the Maori war-effort. In one sense of course this judgement was correct – they could not afford to simply ignore the challenge that they posed nor the hostile forces they sheltered – yet in fact the Maori had little emotional commitment to the fighting *pa*. They built them to provoke a confrontation, and to inflict casualties – and preferably the shame of defeat – upon their enemies; once that had been achieved there was no strategic need to continue to occupy them, and they perceived no shame in abandoning them. Time and again the British expended a tremendous amount of effort and blood in trying to capture a *pa* only to find that the Maori, having achieved their objectives, then abandoned it. It was for this reason, indeed, that most *pa* were built with a sound escape route incorporated into the design. As a result the

The formidable redoubts at the centre of the Rangiriri *pa* in the Waikato, depicted after their capture in November 1863. (Author's collection)

British position before Ruapekepeka, January 1846. The *pa* can be seen in a clearing in the bush on the hillside; the camp of the British and their Maori allies is protected by a similar stockade; artillery and rockets are being fired on the left. (Alexander Turnbull Library, National Library of New Zealand)

balance of victory and defeat in some of the most famous battles of the wars is still open to debate. By the mid-1860s the British had largely become aware that they achieved little by occupying individual *pa*, but as they remained the most tangible expression of Maori defiance they were condemned to attack them anyway.

Conventional British doctrine suggested that emplaced positions should be softened up by an artillery barrage, to destroy fortifications and disable or demoralize the occupants, and then attacked by storming parties directed against any breaches in the walls. In the 1840s the British lacked heavy artillery support, and their bombardments produced little effect on Maori *pa* – although it has been pointed out that to lie in a trench for several hours while round-shot and shell tore through the earth above, knowing that an attack was imminent, required of the defenders an extraordinary degree of courage and determination in itself. The dangers of launching an assault against positions that had not been thoroughly suppressed were obvious enough, yet on several occasions British commanders were prepared to take the risk – often with disastrous results.

At the end of June 1845, for example, Col. Despard bombarded Hone Heke's Ohaeawai *pa* with two 6-pdr and two 12-pdr guns for several days. The bombardment made no apparent impression on the defences and Despard postponed two planned assaults when it became clear that no breach in the palisades had been made. Growing increasingly frustrated, he authorized an assault to take place on 1 July, despite warnings from his Maori allies that Heke's men were still in their positions. An assault column was formed of 220 men of the 58th and 99th regiments supported by sailors and settlers carrying axes and scaling ladders. The storming party crossed several hundred metres of open ground until it reached to within 30m of the *pekerangi* when the defenders loosed a devastating volley from beneath the suspended palings. Although some of the British managed to penetrate the outer palisade they then came under fire from the defenders concealed in trenches within. The attack ground to a halt and the men were recalled having suffered 40 dead and 70 wounded. Ten days after the failed assault Ohaeawai was found to be abandoned.

Similar attacks in later campaigns met with largely the same result. At Puketakauere in the Taranaki on 27 June 1860 350 men, mostly from the 40th Regiment, attacked the *pa* of the Te Atiawa *rangitara* Hapurona. The attack bogged down at the first line of Maori trenches. The British had wisely sent a flanking party to work round the *pa* and cut off the Maori line of retreat but the Maori anticipated the move and caught the attackers in difficult swampy terrain. The assault on Puketakauere proved no more successful than that at Ohaeawai and cost the British 30 dead and 34 wounded, two mortally. At Rangiriri in the Waikato the British enjoyed a significant numerical superiority – some 1,500 men supported by gunboats and artillery – over 500 Maori. The Maori had also constructed outlying rifle pits that commanded the slopes leading down to the Waikato river, from where they expected the British to attack. Although the British commander, General Cameron, was able to land his men at various points to threaten Rangiriri on several sides, the subsequent attack was hardly less of a shambles than its predecessors:

> The ditch, which was dry, was too wide to cross without planks, and the parapet too high (21 ft) to climb without ladders. No such appliances were with the attacking party. About 220 natives held the bastion and traverses about it. They were attacked by a portion of the 65th Regiment who got onto

A sketch of British troops entering Ruapekapeka on 11 January 1846 after it had been abandoned by the defenders. The troops are entering via a breach in the stockade; note also a Maori-style palisade erected to screen the British guns (right). (Alexander Turnbull Library, National Library of New Zealand)

the parapet of the curtain, but were unable to take the bastion. A detail of the Royal Artillery men (36 men) with their carbines then assaulted it. They got up close to the bastion and their commanding officer was mortally wounded and lay close to the rear of the bastion, but they were obliged to retire.

About 90 men of the Naval Brigade then advanced. They got into the ditch, but all attempts to capture the bastion failed. A midshipman, the most advanced, was killed in a covered way that led from the ditch into the interior of the bastion. Though foiled, the sailors did not altogether retire; they scooped out holes and caves in the counterscarp and so sheltered themselves from the enfilading fire from the bastion, and thus remained in close proximity to it all night, occasionally throwing hand grenades amongst the natives.

During the night the assailants made a partial mine under the near face of the bastion, and at daylight on seeing a cask of powder being brought to blow them up, the natives hoisted a white flag and surrendered, 183 in number. Thirty-six natives had been killed.

Two nine-pounder Armstrong guns throwing shells at the bastion made no practical impression on it. A naval six-pounder and two gunboats also fired into it without effect.[14]

At the Gate *pa* on 29 April 1864 the confusion of Maori entrenchments proved just as lethal to the assault parties – exacerbated on this occasion, ironically, by a British success at blocking the Maori escape route. The *pa* itself was a small one – a length of trench 300m long across the neck of a peninsular, reinforced by two strongholds, one 90 by 18m and the other 26 by 18m. There was a light palisade outside the entrenchments front and back. The defenders numbered some 235 men under the command of Puhirake. The British began a bombardment at 7 in the morning and launched an assault at 4 in the afternoon. A party of the 68th Regiment was deployed at the rear of the *pa* while 300 men of the 43rd Regiment and the Naval Brigade rushed the defences from the front. The attackers found that the artillery bombardment had breached the palisade but as they burst through the broken timbers they found themselves under heavy fire from the men lining the trenches within. Several of the officers were shot down – four officers of the 43rd were found dead the following morning lying close together in the breach itself – and the assault began to break up. The men were now exposed in the open within the complex ground and an easy target at point-blank range for the Maori in their trenches

14 Major Charles Heaphy VC, quoted in Parham and Ryan, *The Colonial New Zealand Wars.*

BELOW LEFT
This sketch of an attempt by Captain Mercer and 36 men of the Royal Artillery to storm the entrenchment at Rangiriri on 20 November 1863 suggests just how formidable the *pa* was, despite the lack of any sort of palisade. (Taranaki Museum)

BELOW RIGHT
Aerial photograph of the Orakau site today. (Kevin L Jones/New Zealand Department of Conservation)

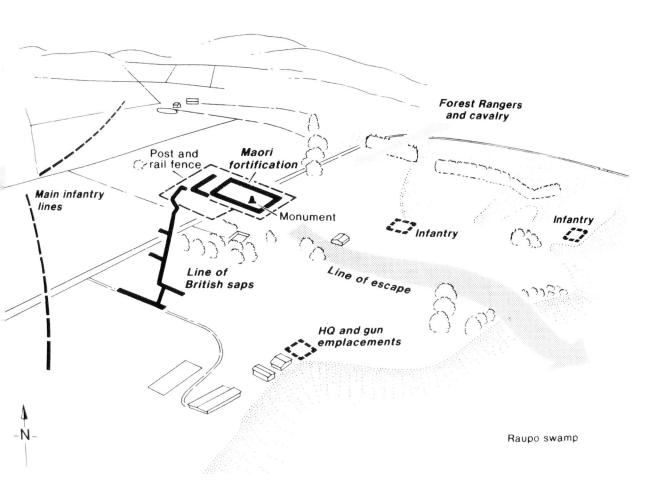

Forest Rangers and cavalry

Post and rail fence

Maori fortification

Main infantry lines

Monument

Infantry

Infantry

Line of British saps

Line of escape

HQ and gun emplacements

-N-

Raupo swamp

all around them. Nevertheless, some Maori began to slip away, only to find their route blocked by the men of the 68th posted in the rear. These Maori turned and rushed back into the trenches, adding to the confusion of the mêlée, and the assault party broke and fled. British casualties amounted to 35 dead and 75 wounded; that night, under cover of pouring rain, most of the Maori slipped through the British lines and escaped.

Even when an assault was successful it could prove almost too costly to justify the objectives achieved. An attack by the 14th and 57th regiments at two different points on the Hau Hau Otopawa *pa* on 14 January 1864 succeeded in penetrating the Maori stockades and entrenchments and forcing the defenders to flee. On this occasion a detachment of Maori fighting with the British caught the Hau Hau as they escaped into the bush and inflicted heavy casualties upon them, but the commander of the 57th, Lieutenant-Colonel Jason Hassard, was wounded while leading a detachment of his men to clear a well-directed cross-fire inflicted on the attackers by Maori concealed in the surrounding bush; Hassard was carried from the field but died of his injuries.

The lessons of such dismal incidents were obvious enough, but the *pa* posed very real military challenges that continued to trouble the British. One solution was to respond to engineering problems with conventional engineering solutions. As early as the assault on Ruapekapeka in 1846 British engineers suggested breaching the palisades by placing charges against them, but in fact it proved impossible to reach close enough to the defences to be able to do so. It was also recognized that the successive lines of fortification

Diagram of the attack on Rewi's *pa* at Orakau, matched to the aerial photograph. (Kevin L Jones/New Zealand Department of Conservation)

49

An aerial view of Rangiriri today. Most traces of the defences have been obliterated but one deep section of trench remains (centre left, near the road junction). (Kevin L Jones/ New Zealand Department of Conservation)

An engraving of the central redoubt of Pukehinahina, the famous Gate *pa*, the scene of a disastrous British repulse on 28 April 1864. The *pa* consisted of a long trench reinforced by two strongpoints and screened by a light palisade. (Author's collection)

would have made any successful detonation of a charge of limited use – it might have made a breach in the outer works, but the assault parties would still have to face the warren of earthworks and stockades beyond. Occasionally attacking parties attempted to set fire to the outer stockades, but they were of course impossibly exposed to the fire of the defenders, who were usually able to extinguish the fire once the attackers had been driven back. An account of the destruction of the Ohaeawai *pa* after it had been evacuated in 1845 in any case gives some insight into the physical difficulties of demolishing such works, even when they were not actively defended:

It occupied us three days to destroy the Ohaeawai *pa*. Large fires were made against the stockade in several places, and where the posts were too thick to burn whilst standing upright, they were pulled down by main force. In some cases it took us the whole strength of forty men, with ropes, to pull down one

LEFT
The attack on the *pa* on Waireka Hill early in the Taranaki campaign earned Leading Seaman William Odgers a Victoria Cross. In fact *pa* of this period seldom had such formidable palisades. (Author's collection)

RIGHT
Rewi Maniapoto, the defender of Orakau *pa,* whose defiance despite being cut off and short of both water and ammunition has come to symbolize the spirit of Maori resistance in the wars of the 1860s. (Author's collection)

BELOW
A plan of Rewi's *pa* at Orakau. (Author's collection)

post, although much of the earth at the base had been previously dug away for the purpose of loosening it.[15]

During the same campaign the British used Congreve rockets fired into the *pa* in the hope of setting fire to the *whares* within. Despite the fact that such rockets were extremely unpredictable in flight, there was some potential for success in this since rockets were perhaps at their most effective as incendiary devices. Nevertheless, the Maori neutralized the danger by piling green flax and soil over vulnerable areas within the stockade.

During the Taranaki campaign of 1860, Major-General Pratt established the precedent of approaching Maori entrenchments by means of a sap – a trench dug towards the enemy to protect the approach of assault parties or to undermine the defences. At the very end of December Pratt advanced on the *pa* of Te Arei, and after clearing away outlying Maori rifle pits began to construct a series of earthwork redoubts to protect his movements. Pratt instructed a detachment of Royal Engineers to begin sapping towards the main work at Te Arei. The sap consisted of a trench deep enough to shelter the occupants, the sides supported with wicker gabions full of earth. At regular intervals traverses were constructed

15 Report from the *United Services Magazine* 1846 quoted in Best, *The Pa Maori.*

PLAN & SECTIONS
OF THE
PAH AT ORAKAU.

Reference.
Parapets
Ditches

SECTION__A. B.

SECTION__C. D.

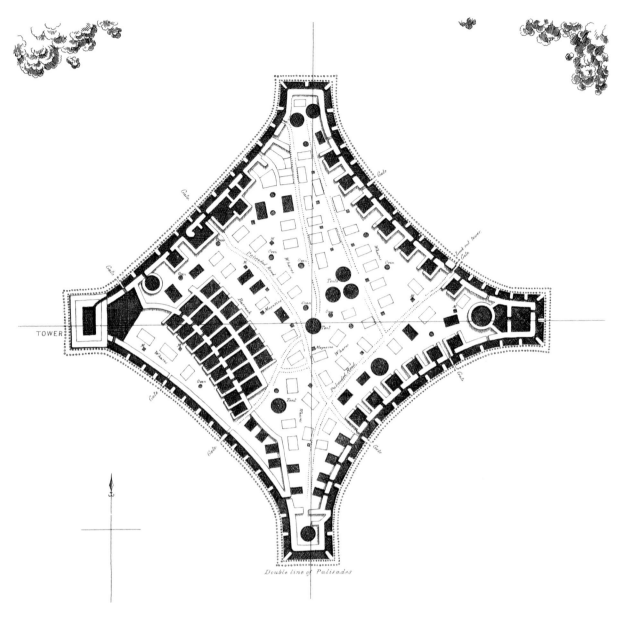

ABOVE
Plan of Titokawaru's famous *pa* at Tauranga-Ika. Although built late in the cycle of Anglo-Maori conflict, 1869, it was still a formidable example of the gunfighters' *pa*. (Author's collection)

RIGHT
Troops attacking Tauranga-Ika in February 1869. The formidable sweep of the palisades, so obvious in profile, can easily be recognized here. (Author's collection)

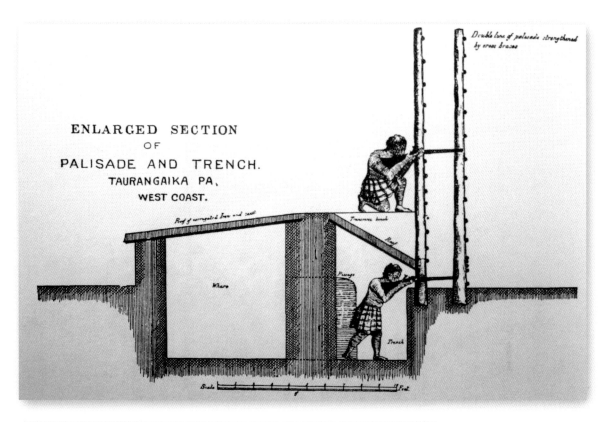

ENLARGED SECTION
OF
PALISADE AND TRENCH.
TAURANGAIKA PA,
WEST COAST.

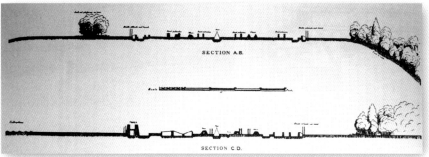

SECTION A.B.

SECTION C.D.

ABOVE
The defences of Tauranga-Ika included a double row of palisades behind which the defenders could fire at ground level from the shelter afforded by a deep ditch. Inside the *pa* were a number of sunken *whares* covered over with corrugated iron, matting and earth to render them shellproof. In some places platforms extended from these buildings to the palisades to provide a second firing line. (Author's collection)

LEFT
Cross section of the defences at Tauranga-Ika. Note how the living quarters were sunk into the ground to provide protection against shellfire. (Author's collection)

across the sap to prevent Maori fire striking down the length of it. At periodic intervals trenches were thrown out on either side to provide cover for parties providing fire support for the sappers. When a secure position was reached Pratt threw up further redoubts to protect the work. Work on the sap was carried out day and night, and the Maori, recognizing the threat it afforded, kept up a constant fire on the men working there and made sorties against the redoubts. The sap extended for over 700m, and was undoubtedly instrumental in persuading the defenders to come to terms before an assault was launched.

Although Pratt was criticized for the cautious nature of his advance – Pratt's Sap was the largest engineering work built in New Zealand by British troops during the wars – he had undeniably achieved his objective, and it is unlikely that Te Arei would have fallen with less loss of British life by any other means. Equally, the garrison would undoubtedly have abandoned it eventually however it had been attacked, denying Pratt, like most British commanders before and after him, the satisfaction of a tangible success.

A sketch of an attack by the 57th Regiment on a Hau Hau *pa* which shows many of the typical elements of such fighting; troops skirmish with Maori defenders in outlying rifle-pits in the foreground while an assault column storms the *pa* behind – and the defenders slip away at the rear. (Author's collection)

Sapping continued to be employed as a technique in later wars. During the attack on Orakau in March 1864 the British constructed a sap leading from their positions to a peach grove close to the Maori lines; this was used to provide a safe communication trench from which troops went forwards to assemble for an assault on the *pa* on 1 April.

Throughout the wars there was a steady improvement in the artillery pieces available to the British, too. The light field pieces of the 1840s made little impression against Heke's and Kawiti's *pa*. In the 1860s the British deployed 12-pdr Armstrong breech-loaders, which had a greater penetrative power, and were occasionally able to call upon heavier Navy guns. The effectiveness of even these, however, could still be countered by digging deeper

D BRITISH COUNTER-ENGINEERING WORKS, BASED ON 'PRATT'S SAP' AT TE AREI, JANUARY–MARCH 1861

The British employed saps – trenches supported by earth-filled gabions and screened by flanking traverses – against several *pa* in the 1860s, most notably at Te Arei. The sap was dug towards the *pa* under cover of fire from men in the traverses – once it reached its target the intention was to undermine the defences of the *pa* or to destroy them with explosives, but in fact most Maori abandoned their positions once the sap reached dangerously close. Although sapping was labour intensive and time consuming, it allowed attackers to reach their objectives with minimal risk from Maori fire. General Pratt's sap at Te Arei was the largest British engineering work built during the New

Zealand Wars, as it was further protected by earthwork redoubts – usually oblong in shape with a projecting bastion at opposite corners – thrown up as it progressed. The Maori attempted to halt the progress of the work by launching surprise attacks upon these redoubts, as here, but they were usually as unable to penetrate the British defences as the British were theirs. Shown inside the defences here is a small Coehorn mortar, which was popular among British and colonial troops in the 1860s as it could be carried by hand through the bush (poles were run through the carriage to make a stretcher) and was effective at lobbing shells over Maori palisades and into the inner trenches.

British counter-engineering works, based on 'Pratt's Sap' at Te Arei, January–March 1861

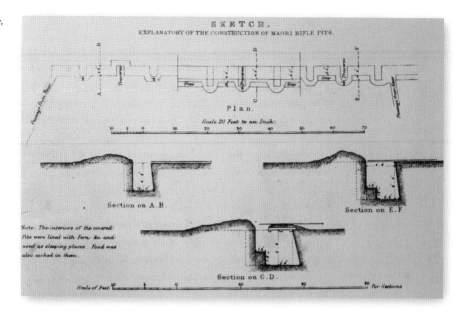

Outlying rifle pits such as these, usually built to screen the approaches to a *pa* and protected by logs overhead, became a feature of Maori fortifications in the 1860s. (Author's collection)

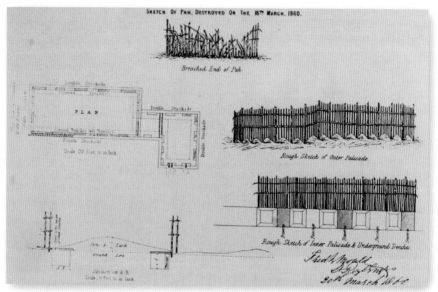

Plan of the Te Kohia *pa* in the Taranaki, captured in March 1860 showing the outer palisade, and the effect of shellfire – which damaged but did not destroy it – upon it. (Author's collection)

and more secure bombproof shelters. Often, when an artillery barrage did play a part in a British victory, it was not so much the physical destruction of the stockades and trenches which was decisive as the psychological strain it imposed upon the defenders, forcing them to live underground, sometimes for days on end, while the shells tore up the ground above them.

Rather more effective was the light 4.4in Coehorn mortar, a short, squat barrel mounted at a fixed angle of 45 degrees on a wooden block carriage. This fired a shell weighing four kilograms and the range was calculated by adjusting the strength of the charge. The high angle of the trajectory meant that shells could be lobbed over the outer palisade and would drop steeply into the entrenchments within. The small bursting charge was compensated for by the fact that the mortar could be carried by hand on a stretcher, making it more portable than guns mounted on conventional wheeled carriages. For this reason it was greatly favoured by colonial troops in the campaigns of the 1860s.

In truth the British never found a single reliable means of dealing with Maori fortifications. They continued to attempt to overcome them by a combination of artillery barrage, engineering and siege techniques and assault, direct or otherwise, throughout 30 years of campaigning. Ultimately, however, it was the steady rise in the number of British troops involved, which allowed them to dominate the landscape and increasingly limit hostile Maori to their strongholds, and their greater reliance on the employment of Maori allies and colonial troops, which swung the military balance gradually in their favour. Whereas in the 1840s British troops, trained to fight in close formations and using cumbersome weapons that were slow to reload, regarded the bush as an entirely impractical environment – thus leaving it to the Maori to exploit to their advantage – the 1860s saw the emergence of local troops prepared to fight the Maori on their own ground. These included allied Maori and settler units, such as the Forest Rangers or the New Zealand Armed Constabulary. The British were also prepared to wage a more ruthless type of war, destroying the homes and crops of Maori groups not directly involved in the fighting so as to deny logistical support to warriors in the field. In battle such troops were used to clear the bush surrounding a *pa* as a preliminary to an assault, and where possible to surround it and cut off any line of retreat. If the British commander had sufficient patience this sometimes

ABOVE
An aerial photo of the Ngatapa site that clearly demonstrates its natural inaccessibility. (Kevin L Jones/New Zealand Department of Conservation)

BELOW
Sketch of the defences of the Ngatapa *pa* built by Te Kooti in the Poverty Bay area in late 1868. The *pa* was built on a high plateau with limited approach routes; these were screened by several rows of trenches. In fact the position could not be held indefinitely because it had only limited access to water. (Kevin L Jones/New Zealand Department of Conservation)

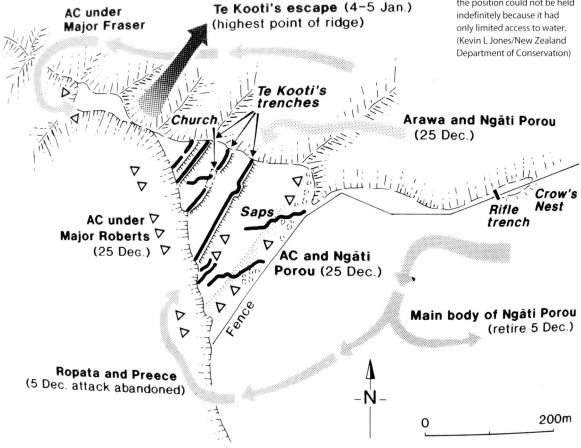

An aerial photograph of Pratt's Sap, the long trench, screened by traverses and parallel supporting trenches, by which the British captured the Te Arei *pa* in 1860 Although the use of saps was controversial – because of the effort it entailed – it usually forced the Maori to surrender their works without the need for a costly frontal assault. (Kevin L Jones/ New Zealand Department of Conservation)

produced results in itself; invested garrisons sometimes capitulated as their supplies of food, ammunition and water gave out, and once it became clear that they could not evacuate their positions if they chose. More often, it simply became important to dominate the surrounding bush in order to make it possible to assemble an assault party in safety as close to the stockades as possible. It is no coincidence that the fighting which accompanied the assaults upon Titokawaru's Te Ngutu o te Manu *pa* in August and September 1868 was largely carried out among the surrounding bush rather than on the palisades themselves. It is also worth noting that, despite the general ascendancy of colonial forces by this stage, these attacks ended in failure and led to the death of the noted forest fighter Major Gustavus von Tempsky.

E AN ATTACK ON A GUNFIGHTERS' *PA*, C.1866.

The classic late New Zealand War-period *pa* included a single or double wooden stockade – much smaller and lighter than in pre-European times – which was defended by means of interior trenches. This pa has a double stockade, and the outer trench lies between the two rows of stakes – the defenders fired through loopholes in the palisade at ground level to provide a curtain of fire which was devastating at close quarters. The defenders are shown here in late war-costume – a mix of traditional items and European clothing (shirts and waist-cloths). Many Maori at this time carried flintlock or percussion muskets or double-barrelled shotguns, although traditional weapons and iron-bladed hatchets were popular for close-quarter fighting. Once the outer palisade had been taken particularly determined defenders could still hold the inner line; the gateway between the palisades was usually carefully screened, as in the foreground here. Any attack that attempted to storm the gateway would be channelled down a narrow rat-run and exposed to fire along the length of it from defenders on the other side of the stakes. Here the attackers – wearing the typical blue field uniforms adopted by British troops in New Zealand in the 1860s – are exploiting a lucky breach made by artillery fire in the outer stockade; most *pa* of this period were provided with sheltered escape routes (left) through which the defenders could evacuate the position when hard pressed. Such *pa* were built with specific tactical purposes in mind – usually to draw an enemy attack and inflict as many casualties as possible – and it was not necessary to hold them indefinitely once those objectives had been achieved.

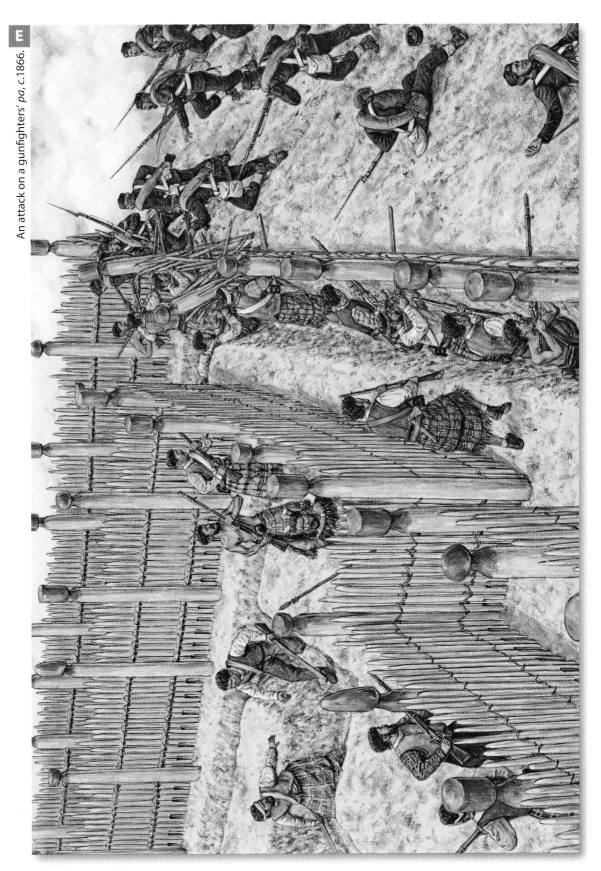

An attack on a gunfighters' pa, c.1866.

THE END OF THE *PA*

The Maori remained committed to the concept of the *pa* until the very end of the New Zealand Wars; Titokawaru's Taugranga-Ika was as impressive and complex as almost anything built since the 1840s. Judged on its own terms, the *pa* had been a resounding success. It had consistently allowed the Maori to control the strategic initiative, dictating the pace and place of conflict, and the fact that all *pa* were eventually abandoned to, or captured by, the enemy does not detract from the damage and embarrassment inflicted consistently on the British.

In the end, however, the *pa* became obsolete in the face of the inexorable settler domination of New Zealand itself. Land was confiscated from Maori groups accused of complicity in resistance, chiefs and their warriors were captured or killed, and the ability of the Maori community to sustain their men on campaign undermined. By contrast the numbers of British troops and later colonial militias steadily increased, and the weapons and techniques available to them improved. By the late 1860s it was clear not so much that *pa* could be any more easily taken, but that the Maori could not defend them indefinitely in an environment now dominated by their enemies.

Nevertheless, even Te Kooti, the last great war leader to emerge in the fighting, whose skills lay rather in his ability to move his small band of followers quickly through inhospitable terrain, and to mount quick, unexpected and ruthless attacks, built a *pa* at Te Porere in September 1869. The *pa* was built on a high point with a much smaller out-work on a knoll lower down. The *pa* lacked the complex web of entrenchments that characterized successful works of the period, and indeed seems to have been influenced by European military redoubts, incorporating as it did a basically square design with two corner bastions. The *pa* was attacked by a combined Constabulary and Maori force on 4 October 1869 who drove Te Kooti's men from the outlying works and then successfully stormed the main position killing 37 men and taking 30 women and children prisoner.

Te Kooti himself escaped, and did not again rely upon earthworks to defend himself. The action at Te Porere was the last Maori defence of a *pa* during the New Zealand Wars.

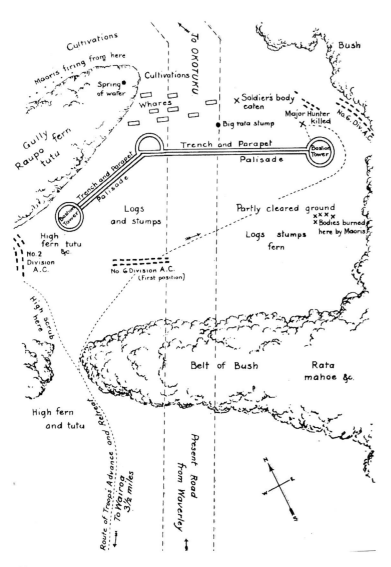

PA SITES TODAY

The Maori built many thousands of fortified villages in New Zealand, mainly in the North Island, between their arrival in the 13th century and 1869. While the wooden palisading which was such a feature of their construction has long since gone, there are numerous remains visible. Ironically, in many cases old sites, where the *pa* was constructed on an inaccessible hilltop, have tended to survive rather better than those constructed to defend the islands against the *pakeha*. There are several reasons for this, not least that older *pa* often in any case left more significant physical remains – deeper trenches and higher ramparts – while the land which they occupied has been less in demand in the years since for commercial agriculture. *Pa* built in the 1860s, in particular, were often constructed on ground desired by European settlers – much of it flat and easy to plough – and after their capture and the subsequent confiscation of tribal land, they were often destroyed by farming activity. Some, indeed, were destroyed even during the war years; since many were built on good

The Te Porere *pa* built by Te Kooti in September 1869. Te Kooti was primarily a guerrilla leader and this *pa*, which owed much to the design of British and colonial redoubts, was captured by assault on 4 October. It proved to be the last Maori fortification built during the New Zealand Wars. (Kevin L Jones/New Zealand Department of Conservation)

strategic positions, it was quite common for the troops who captured them to build their own redoubts on the same spot, sometimes utilizing or converting the existing earthworks. This occurred in the case of the Gate *pa*, when troops destroyed the Maori works to build a fortified post shortly after the battle. On other occasions, once fighting ceased and Europeans had pacified an area, Christian churches were sometimes built on *pa* sites, both to honour those who died attacking and defending them, and as a mark of the displacement of Maori tradition by settler society. Many *pa* have indeed been obliterated by subsequent urban development. This is the case at Ohaeawai, Matai-Taua and Tauranga-Ika. Indeed, the remains of many British entrenchments seem to have survived rather better than those of the Maori whose lands they were invading.

Nonetheless, some impressive remains do survive and Nigel Prickett's *Landscapes of Conflict; A Field Guide to the New Zealand Wars* (Auckland, 2002) is an essential guide for anyone interested in investigating them further. Ruapekepeka, Kawiti's famous *pa* of 1846, now lies within a protected Historic Reserve. Although modern access roads frame it on two sides, the depressions marking the outline of the perimeter, and the shelters within, have all been remarkably well preserved. In the middle of the *pa* stands a carronade which had belonged to Heke before the war, and which was disabled by a British shell; the damage can clearly be seen in its shattered barrel. The sites of British positions nearby are also preserved. Of the 1860s battlefields, a section of Pratt's Sap at Te Arei in the Taranaki has survived in the Pukerangiora Historic Reserve, but while faint traces of the supporting redoubts can sometimes be seen in the fields of privately owned neighbouring farmland, few traces remain of the *pa* itself. Despite considerable development around and among them, however, some traces of the formidable Rangiriri earthworks have survived and a small interpretation centre serves these. The site of Titokawaru's famous

A Maori war-dance or *peru peru* as depicted in a 19th-century engraving. The background gives a good impression of the interior of a pre-colonial *pa*; note the *whares*, or living houses, and the high palisade beyond. (Author's collection)

Te Ngutu o te Manu *pa* is marked by a monument, but now lies within a recreational campsite. Ironically, much of Te Kooti's *pa* at Te Porere still remains intact. Of other famous sites, much more famous in their day, such as the Gate *pa* and Orakau, nothing remains but monuments marking their locations, some of them lying incongruously now along pleasant suburban lanes.

FURTHER READING

Until the middle of the 20th century the New Zealand Wars had remained largely the preserve of military men writing their memoirs or of historians working within an essentially British or colonial framework. Since the 1950s a strong revisionist tradition has emerged, however, some of it reflecting the perceptions of the Maori community for whom the wars, and the issue of land ownership resulting from them, remain politically sensitive.

A good place to start any exploration of this complex subject is *The Colonial New Zealand Wars* by Tim Ryan and Bill Parham (Grantham House, Wellington, 1986), which provides a profusely illustrated introduction to both the fighting and the military techniques employed by both sides. Of the older histories, James Cowan's *The New Zealand Wars*, first published in 1922/23 (Government Printer, Wellington), remains invaluable both for the sheer scope of the material included, and for his willingness to listen to sources from both sides. It is ideally read alongside James Belich's impressive revisionist work of the same name (Auckland University Press, Auckland, 1986), which evaluates the fighting in a broader context. Belich is also the author of an excellent study of one of the last campaigns, *I Shall Not Die; Titokawaru's War* (Allan and Unwin, Wellington, 1989). Michael Barthorp's *To Face the Daring Maoris* (Hodder and Stoughton, London, 1979) provides an eyewitness history of the Northern War of the 1840s, based heavily upon British soldiers' accounts.

For Maori fortifications, Elsdon Best's *The Pa Maori*, first published in 1927 (Dominion Museum, Wellington), remains the standard history, providing remarkable detail of the construction techniques, particularly of the pre-colonial era. Best regarded the gunfighters' *pa* as the end of the golden age of Maori military engineering, but his descriptions remain essential reading. Nigel Prickett's *Landcapes of Conflict; A Field Guide to the New Zealand Wars* (Random House, Auckland, 2002) provides an excellent summary of the wars against an illustrated backdrop depicting the sites then and now.

GLOSSARY

Ariki	The male representative of a senior lineage within the *iwi* – a chief.
Hapu	a sub-group within the tribe (*iwi*) usually based upon extended kinship.
Iwi	the tribe, consisting of a number of *hapu*.
Kahia	human figures carved into principle stockade posts.
Mana	the spiritual manifestation of on individual's personal power, prestige and influence.
Ngutu	narrow entrance to a stockade, often screened.
Rangatira	the male heads of senior lineages within the *hapu*, sub-chiefs.
Pa	a defensive position made by a combination of entrenchments or palisades.
Parakiri	innermost line of a stockade.
Pekerangi	the outer screen or stockade of a *pa*.
Pourewa	elevated fighting platform.
Toa	a Maori warrior.
Tuwatawata	third line of a stockade.
Utu	payment or revenge exacted for a slight.
Waha	entrance or gateway.
Whare	home or dwelling hut.
Wita	second line of a stockade.

INDEX

References to illustrations are shown in bold.
Plates are shown with page and caption
locators in brackets.